PENGUIN BOOKS

THE IDEA OF ECONOMIC COMPLEXITY

David Warsh writes on economics for the *Boston Globe*. A graduate of Harvard College, he covered the Vietnam war for *Pacific Stars and Stripes* and *Newsweek*, and reported business for *The Wall Street Journal* and *Forbes*. In 1977 he received the Loeb Award for National Magazine Writing for the article that was the genesis of this book. He lives with his wife and children in Somerville, Massachusetts.

THE IDEA OF
ECONOMIC COMPLEXITY

DAVID WARSH

PENGUIN BOOKS

PENGUIN BOOKS

Viking Penguin Inc., 40 West 23rd Street, New York, New York 10010, U.S.A.
Penguin Books Ltd, Harmondsworth, Middlesex, England
Penguin Books Australia Ltd, Ringwood, Victoria, Australia
Penguin Books Canada Limited, 2801 John Street, Markham, Ontario, Canada L3R 1B4
Penguin Books (N.Z.) Ltd, 182–190 Wairau Road, Auckland 10, New Zealand

First published in the United States of America by Viking Penguin Inc. 1984
Published in Penguin Books 1985

LIBRARY OF CONGRESS CATALOGING IN PUBLICATION DATA
Warsh, David.
The idea of economic complexity.
Bibliography: p.
Includes index.
1. Inflation (Finance)   2. Prices.   3. Cost and standard of living.   I. Title.
HG229.W34   1985   339.4'2   85-9291
ISBN 0 14 00.8099 6

Printed in the United States of America by
R. R. Donnelley & Sons Company, Harrisonburg, Virginia
Set in Plantin Roman

Charts by Anita Giraldo
Copyright © Viking Penguin Inc., 1984

PREFACE

A BOOK WITH A TITLE AS BALD AS THIS ONE REQUIRES A WORD OF explanation. Why would anyone want to read it? The reason is that the idea of economic complexity can change forever the way you think about the cost of living. If you ever wonder why $10 doesn't go very far in the shops today (when it was a great deal of money fifty years ago), then this book is worth reading. You don't need any special knowledge of economics in order to enjoy it; a curiosity about our world is enough.

There is an ancient debate among experts about the cause of the persistently rising prices that we have experienced since the eve of World War II. Is "inflation" the result of an overblown money supply, as some economists insist? Or, as many other economists insist, is it precipitated by the actions of organizations such as the Organization of Petroleum Exporting Countries (OPEC), big governments, big unions, and big companies, which call more money into existence mostly as a side effect? And if the pushing and jostling behavior of groups is responsible for rising prices, as so many people believe to be the case, do these pushes have anything in common with each other? Or are they autonomous and disparate events, deserving to be called "special factors"? For a decade, this controversy between "structuralists" and "monetarists" was couched in terms of "cost-push" versus "demand-pull" inflation; now the concept of "supply shock" has replaced "cost push" and confused the issue. But the question remains unresolved, and part of the reason is that the "one big idea" of the money supply versus "a lot of little things" of the structuralists confers an extraordinary theoretical advantage on the monetarists.

The idea of economic complexity offers a way to go beyond the familiar relationship between prices and money to seek a glimpse of the circumstances that govern the creation of money. Everyone can agree, I think, that governments and banks have a far-reaching power to create money and so to affect economic activity; to put it more concretely, what the Board of Governors of the Federal Reserve System does matters a great deal. But nearly everyone except a few monetarists can also agree that the conduct of monetary policy by the Fed is not all that matters. Economic complexity is a unifying conception that allows us to talk about many diverse elements of economic structure that are often blamed for rising prices, from interest group politics to technical change. As an aspect of the division of labor, complexity is rooted deep in our sense of what constitutes an economy; it is consensible, resonant, concrete. The idea that complexity is a measurable, objective dimension of economic systems may be hard to fathom initially, but after a little practice, it will become a useful intuitive concept whose measurement may be left to experts, just like M1, productivity gain, or the GNP.

To be sure, what is contained in the middle chapters of this book isn't a *theory* of rising prices at all. It is stretching the point to call it a hypothesis. The proposition that the prices we pay are higher because we are buying a more complex bundle of goods is a glimpse of a concept that eventually may offer common ground for a wide range of economists who now march under the "institutionalist" banner—and a painful choice for those who think of themselves as Keynesians.

It is not altogether easy for a journalist, especially one who covers economics, to report the existence of a previously unremarked major macroeconomic variable, even if this variable is one that most people already comprehend intuitively. Economists mustn't be expected to welcome the news. From a technical point of view, this account of it is underargued, to say the least; but the point, after all, is to spark discussion: if it calls into being a hundred essays on economic complexity, it will have done its work. This isn't the last word on the subject of economic complexity; it is the first. It isn't economics; it's news.

I came to this project with the usual reporter's tools, skepticism, and background knowledge. The background in this case was supplied by my undergraduate experience in the social studies program at Harvard College. It was in conversations with E. Lawrence Minard, Margaret Everett, Paul Blustein, John Hotson, George Gilder, and Peter Albin that my ideas about complexity developed. A large number of scholars, in conversation and correspondence, helped me to sharpen my views and to understand their possibilities and limitations, and though I will try to repay their various kindnesses through citation, this cannot compensate them fairly for the time they took, for the etiquette of citation in journalism is quite different from what it is in scholarship.

Several editors wrestled with my attempts to set down what I saw along the way, including James Michaels, Sheldon Zelaznick, Midge Decter, David Ewing, Roy Rotheim, and Robert Kuttner, and even when they were unsuccessful in committing me to print, I learned from them a great deal about the nature of the enterprise. It was William Strachan, my fellow midwesterner, who finally succeeded. Leslie Lenkowsky and Randy Richardson played an important role in developing my views, even when neither particularly agreed with them, and I am very grateful for their assistance.

At the *Boston Globe*, I am indebted for advice and encouragement to Robert Phelps, Michael Janeway, and Michael Larkin; to business editor Gordon McKibben for permitting me to arrange my work in such a way as to take advantage of my extracurricular interests; to Ken Lord for offering a congenial place on his sports desk at which to work; and to systems editor Charles Liftman for technical assistance at every turn. I must say a word about the *Globe* itself: it is an extraordinary newspaper, perhaps the only one at which a project such as this could have been accommodated. Mark Feeney, Peter Albin, Sidney Schoeffler, John Case, Mark Silk, Lawrence Minard, and Arthur Hepner read parts of the manuscript with tact and good cheer, and each saved me from errors and tried to save me from sins that I preferred to commit; Feeney in particular influenced the architecture of the book. The manuscript benefited from a careful reading by Kenneth Lane and from the heavy eyeball of Luise Erdmann. I owe special thanks to Ruth Wenner, John Brockman, Rod and Isabelle Gander, Michael and Sandy Marsh, Annis Warsh, and Stephen Warsh. The Newtowne School was a constant source of inspiration and anecdote—often a more than sufficient source. My wife, Hope Tompkins, and our daughters, Molly and Lucy, lived and thrived and made life rich and complex throughout, and they may now enjoy the satisfactions of having completed a difficult job. Hope's faith and charity toward the project cannot be overstated; her influence can be found on every page.

A word about values may be in order. Others have written about economic complexity, and their politics are often quite different from mine. My sentiments are of the sort usually described as liberal, meaning anticorporate. They were confirmed during the four years I spent living in a planned society, and a reasonably well planned one at that—the United States Navy. While the experience erased the great fear that some suffer at the thought of central planning—life in the fleet had its points, after all—it also gave me a healthy appreciation of the joys of living in a decentralized, market-oriented society, in which the phrase "on the outside" has meaning. But just because I like markets doesn't mean that everything reminds me of one.

Somerville, Massachusetts
February 29, 1984

CONTENTS

CONTENTS

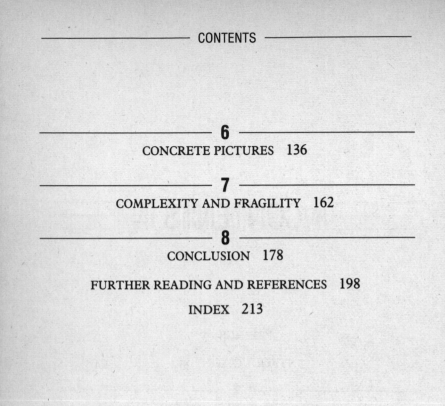

INTRODUCTION

TO BE COMPLEX IS TO CONSIST OF TWO OR MORE SEPARABLE, ANalyzable parts, so the degree of complexity of an economy consists of the number of different kinds of jobs in the system and the manner of their organization and interdependence in firms, industries, and so forth. Economic complexity is reflected, crudely, in the Yellow Pages, by occupational dictionaries, and by standard industrial classification (SIC) codes. It can be measured by sophisticated modern techniques, such as graph theory or automata theory. The whys and wherefores of complexity measurement are not our subject here, however; it is with the idea itself that we are concerned. A high degree of complexity is what hits you in the face in a walk across New York City; it is what is missing in Dubuque, Iowa. A higher degree of specialization and interdependence—not merely more money or greater wealth—is what makes the world of 1984 so different from the world of 1939.

Today there is a great deal of talk about a "new industrial revolution." Computers and biotechnology are going to make the world rich beyond the dreams of avarice, transform the nature of work, or produce unprecedented unemployment—perhaps all three, depending on who is talking. Then again, maybe the revolution is nearly over; only a few years ago all the talk was of the "governmental revolution." Clearly the international division of labor is changing. It would help to be able to measure these things, or at least to be able to talk more clearly about the increasing different-partedness and interdependence—the complexity—of the modern world.

Is the idea of economic complexity a practical matter for the everyday reader? Of course it is. A better understanding of the forces that shape the world is always practical. As George Shackle says, "Theory is the root of peace." I don't think that you will necessarily become a better investor for coming to grips with economic complexity (though you may), but I do think you'll understand far better why in "inflationary" times you cannot relax. I don't think that the next presidential election will find candidates campaigning under pro- and anti-complexity banners; but I do think that for the next fifty years politics will revolve around the issues presented here. I don't think that you will achieve the sort of peace associated with a spiritual discipline by mastering this book; but you will understand far better than before why $10 used to be a lot of money and why it doesn't go far today—and why it isn't a simple matter to reverse this. The increasing complexity of the world has important consequences for our lives.

Economists have only the haziest terms for discussing and analyzing complexity. They speak of "industrialization," "urbanization," and "development," about "structural" and "institutional" change, but these processes are assumed not to be susceptible to measurement. They also have descriptive phrases, such as "managerial revolution," "post-industrial society," "the rise of the public sector," and "the emergence of the service economy." And they have technical terms for dealing with the inescapable ramifications of complexity, such as "the index number problem," "technical change," and even "roundaboutness." But for the purposes of comparing economic systems over time, scholars offer only concepts such as "gross national product per capita," rates of "unemployment," and "inflation." These are useful and important but finally unenlightening concepts when it comes to discussing degrees of specialization and interdependence. It is true that economic complexity will not submit to what economists like to call "the measuring rod of money," but that is no reason to exclude it from what we consider the proper sphere of economics.

Indeed, to think about economic complexity is to participate in an old tradition in economics, for complexity is an attribute of the overall division of labor in society. It entails the degree of specialization not only of a single enterprise—an automobile assembly line or a pin factory or a bank—but of all the tasks in a system, whether the system is a city, a nation, a group of nations, or the world. Complexity is a matter of the number of different kinds of niches, of specialized jobs. Do you believe, like Karl Marx or Jean-Paul Sartre, that specialization should be abolished? Economic complexity is the fly in your ointment, for it is something that, barring nuclear war or an epidemic of vast proportions, will not only not go away but will continue to grow. Do you think, like Adam Smith, that complexity in the division of labor is something that can or should only arise from markets? Then you've got some explaining to do. What about the Soviet Union? Anybody who has ever been to Moscow knows that that city is not negligible in its complexity, though it is not nearly so complex as New York.

Complexity is the key to understanding an economic revolution, for what is such a revolution but a measurable, swift increase in the array of different niches in some part of the economy? Often such a revolution involves simplifying a task once difficult. The air transport revolution, for example, made going to California from New York a relatively simple undertaking, but it also made the transportation industry more complex. We may speak of the revolutions in health care, weaponry, energy provision, information systems, meat packing, and timekeeping, and in each case we mean the same thing. We are talking about the invention of kinds of jobs, of niches. Taken together, they add up to—what? That is what this book is about.

Economists aren't very interested in complexity because of the intellectual tools they acquire with their training—the tools that in effect *are* their training. The very techniques that permit them to be so clear on some subjects cause them to veer off on others. A case in point is the General Equilibrium Theory, in which the world is seen as a system of contending forces of human effort and desire that annihilate each other through the workings of the market. Another is the Quantity Theory of Money, in which economic complexity is conveniently but tacitly assumed to be unchanging. Each of these intellectual lenses tends to focus attention on something other than complexity.

Take the General Equilibrium Theory, for example. General Equilibrium is the name for the edifice of thought, intricate as a cathedral, that surrounds our knowledge of the system by which the prices and quantities of all goods bought and sold are regulated through a kind of continuous auction. If the buyers want more of an item than the suppliers provide, the price rises; the quantity demanded then falls and the quantity offered rises. The converse also holds true. This famous equation between supply and demand, with price as the fulcrum through which balance is attained, is the basis of all that is most familiar in economics. There is not much room for complexity in a view that stresses the canceling out of the countervailing forces of effort and desire, however, for what does the complexity of a system matter if the significant fact about it is its internal balance, or equilibrium? Complexity has to do with the "different-partedness" of the world; supply and demand have to do with the cohesion of its parts, however many there are. Complexity adds up; equilibrium nets out.

Nor can talk about changing degrees of economic complexity be easily accommodated by the worldview implicit in the Quantity Theory of Money. This theory states that the cost of living is a matter of the proportion between the supply of money and the supply of goods in the world, that inflation is "too much money chasing too few goods," that rising prices mean we pay "a great deal more money for the same old things." Since quantity theorists believe that changes "on the side of money" rather than "on the side of goods" are responsible for rising prices, they have come up with a battery of sophisticated techniques for factoring out the inescapable effects of changes on the side of goods, which they regard as a "measurement problem" or just so much "noise."

The idea of economic complexity enters as an attempt to pick up the other end of the stick. To speak of complexity is to describe the underlying changes that take place in the organization of the division of labor, in what economists habitually describe as the "real" economy, then to relate events in the "nominal" economy of prices and money to these changes. In fact, the heart of the book is a proposition about the money cost of living that is designed to compete with the Quantity Theory. The complexity hypothesis, if I may call it that, suggests that the purchasing power of money—and the quantity of money itself—depend fundamentally on the complexity of the economic system in which the money is spent. Steadily rising prices should not be interpreted, as they usually are, to mean that we are getting nothing more for our money, but rather to mean that we are buying a new and more complicated bundle of goods and services, often including many things that are apparently quite unrelated to the products for which we pay. Complexity is not the only thing that affects prices and is often not the most important thing. But as a way of organizing our thinking about the changing cost of living, the concept of complexity is a very valuable tool.

Does this sound difficult? It may be illustrated very simply. Imagine two restaurants. Let one be a simple lunch counter with the usual furnishings: a Formica counter, a waitress, a cook behind a grill, and a menu consisting largely of hamburgers and spaghetti. Let the other be a fancy downtown spot, with tablecloths, fresh flowers on the table, and a menu in French. Now imagine an order for a certain kind of lunch, a "consumption bundle" to an economist: a bowl of soup, a sandwich, a drink, and dessert. What will lunch cost in each restaurant? Suppose that it's $8 at the lunch counter and $20 at the fancy place. Why are prices higher in the second restaurant? What determines the purchasing power of money in these restaurants? The answer has nothing to do with the quantity of money in each restaurant, though there probably is more money in customers' pockets in the fancy place than in the plain one: people bring thick wallets to fancy restaurants because they expect high prices; prices are not high because people bring thick wallets. The real reason for the difference in the cost has to do with the difference in the array of goods and services that are bundled into the menu prices and offered for sale in the two restaurants—in other words, differences in the restaurants' complexity. This is the hypothesis about the relationship among complexity, prices, and money at its simplest. The price of the basics depends on the frills.*

In terms of the complexity hypothesis, urban complexity is a significant reason for the higher cost of living in the city than in the country—and for the greater quantity of money in a city than in a village. Regional complexity is the underlying (although certainly not the only) reason for the greater purchasing power of the dollar in the Sunbelt than in the Northeast. Different degrees of national economic complexity are the basic reason behind the lower costs of making steel in Korea than in Germany, although clearly many other factors enter into the comparison. And economic complexity, rather than a loose hand on the money supply, is at the root of much of the "inflation" of the past fifty years. Instead of "prices and progress," it is "progress and prices"; instead of the social consequences of inflation, it is the price consequences of social processes. The

---

* What about a fast-food restaurant like McDonald's, where specialization results in lower instead of higher prices? The answer is that complexity has more than one aspect. See Chapter 2.

world of 1984 is to the world of 1939 as the fancy restaurant is to the plain one. It is economically more complex.

There is more to this enterprise than simply turning the Quantity Theory on its head, however, for in its very language the Quantity Theory captures the debate. How can we see the growing complexity of the economy with a theory that lets us see only the "inflation" of the money supply? "Too much money chasing too few goods" may be a soothing explanation of events long ago and far away. But when it is used to explain the difference in price levels between our two restaurants, it falls flat; a French restaurant is not a more expensive place than a lunch counter because there are "too many dollars chasing too little food." It is no more helpful to say that prices in the world of 1984 are "inflated" with respect to those of 1939 than it is to say that prices in the fancy restaurant are "inflated" versions of the plain prices. To do so is to inject value judgments into what should be a matter of description. Worse yet is that the term "inflated" is actively misleading, for if you look for money, you miss complexity. What the situation requires is a new vocabulary that permits us to talk clearly about the effects of growing complexity.

I'm sometimes asked how I can have so little to say about the work that has been done by the distinguished economists whose names are familiar to many readers. What about Wassily Leontief, whose input-output tables have spurred the collection of data on the complexity of the economy more than any other tradition? What about the sturdy anti-monetarist theorizing of Paul Davidson and Basil Williams? What about the brilliant critiques of the General Equilibrium concept by Janos Kornai and Nicholas Georgescu-Roegen? What about the analysis of the last fifty years of John Kenneth Galbraith, who may be the best "institutional" economic scholar since Karl Marx? And what about Marx himself?

The answer must be that we are operating at a level deep down, far from policy, most often in the realm of the "pure," and that the concept of complexity is so radical a departure from the usual ways of theorizing that there are relatively few senior workers in the field. For all the empirical spin they impart to research, input-output tables remain a form of equilibrium analysis, characterized by the "netting out" of countervailing forces. For all their insight, the "post-Keynesians" are still linguistic captives of the Quantity Theory. I suppose complexity is basically a Marxist category, though it bears little relation to most of what has been done in that tradition. It is to the work of historians of particular kinds of division of labor—to historians of science (like Thomas Kuhn), of business (like Alfred Chandler), and of economic organization generally (like Fernand Braudel)—that I want to direct attention. The scientific, theoretical counterparts to this book—the work of Kornai, Georgescu-Roegen, and particularly Peter Albin—are terribly abstract and obscure in comparison. I have been able to build only a very few bridges to their thought, though it is obvious that the potential exists for many more connections.

For a professional economist, I must acknowledge that the prospect for irritation here is very great. Economics swept past elementary considerations about the division of labor decades, even centuries, ago, and the considerations here must seem clumsy indeed to those athletes of the mind who are trained in modern modeling techniques. I urge such readers to think of this book as an essay in a peculiar form of sociology and to approach it sideways, a little bit at a time. Indeed, I volunteer a short checklist of the questions that I believe an economist must answer for himself before turning away.

1. Does economic complexity exist? Does a statement such as "The complexity of economic organization has increased since World War II" have meaning?

2. Does complexity have any economic significance at all? Can it increase (or decrease) substantially with *no* economic effects?

3. Does complexity have *any* systematic effects on the "gen-

eral price level"? Can the effect of burgeoning complexity on prices be ascribed only to "nonstandard" economic situations such as health care or defense? Or is the phenomenon to be found more generally?

4. Does complexity have the grand "way of seeing" property that I claim for it? Can a particular case of rising prices (Weimar, say, or the sixteenth-century price explosion) be seen as a matter of increasing money *and* as a matter of complexity and money together? Or does one way of seeing ultimately take precedence over the other?

While I have great hopes for the idea of economic complexity, they are not boundless. I certainly do not believe that it has much of anything to tell us about why bread is cheap and butter dear or a host of other interesting and significant issues. With respect to the "many other factors" that are mentioned with monotonous regularity throughout this book, I can only beg patience. Any writer on economics depends on the goodwill and cooperation of his readers, and anyone who is determined to find fault can raise hundreds of legitimate and yet finally unimportant objections. This is especially true in this case, because the idea of economic complexity is located in a very difficult part of the architecture of economics, being on the one hand at least as generally interesting as the quantity of money, on the other failing to "explain" everything—or, in the end, even to explain very much. It is simply an aspect of things.

I've tried to make the argument about economic complexity ladder-like; that is, I've shown in Chapter 1 something of what is meant generally by the concept of complexity; in Chapter 2, what might be meant by *economic* complexity. In Chapter 3, I have pointed out what I hope are clear and indisputable instances of the way that greater economic complexity and higher prices go hand in hand—health care and defense- and energy-related areas. Some will think that these are "nonstandard" economic situations, in which "soft budget constraints" are at work. I think these patterns are as standard as, say, the corn-hog cycle, through which the effects of information lags on economic performance are explained in every elementary economic text. At any rate, they require recognition.

Only in Chapter 4 have I pressed my claim that complexity is an alternative "way of seeing" to the Quantity Theory. It is here that I pay special attention to the very long-term history of prices in England and to the rival accounts of it given by the Quantity Theory and the complexity hypothesis—a case in which I believe the complexity hypothesis is especially suggestive. The power of this record to inform rests on the existence of a handful of dominating episodes requiring a common explanation.

In the accounts usually given, the present forty-year bout of continuous "inflation" is described as being unprecedented. When data representing "the price level" are displayed graphically, they fluctuate like a sine wave—up-down, up-down, up-down—for two hundred or even three hundred years, before beginning in 1939 a mysterious upward journey that still has not come to an end. The implication is that either the cost of living may be expected to return to historic low levels—the nickel beer will come again—or that something utterly unexpected is going on.

Quite a different expectation emerges from a consideration of the very long-term history of prices. The seven-hundred-year price index that is discussed in Chapter 4 was published twenty-five years ago in a scholarly journal in England by Sir Henry Phelps Brown and Sheila V. Hopkins. In their data, the history of the price level in England looks like a set of stairs drawn by a shaky hand: there are three long periods of continuously rising prices—"price explosions," historians call them—that are unreversed, separated by equally long periods of relative stability in the cost of living. The point is that there are precedents for the explosion of prices that has occurred since World War II—and there is much reason, on the surface at least, to expect the explosion to end ultimately, the cost of living to stabilize, and prices to level off on a new plateau.

The story in this book is thus not the conventional one of governmental efficacy—of fools, rascals, and great men—in which everything in the economy was fine until the Vietnam War, at the conclusion of which the OPEC nations took over the mischief, with a resolute Paul Volcker finally applying the monetary brakes to the banking system in the nick of time. All of this is true and useful as far as it goes, but it doesn't go far enough. For if it was Paul Volcker who stopped "inflation" in the 1980s, who was it who stopped a century of unreversed "inflation" in the 1640s? Oliver Cromwell?

The explanation usually offered for unreversed price explosions has to do with money. Thus, in the words of the Quantity Theory of Money, "Inflation is too much money chasing too few goods." The Quantity Theory holds broadly that it was New World gold and silver that caused the unreversed "inflation" in the sixteenth century; that the widespread adoption of paper money was the culprit in the eighteenth century; and that credit cards and their sophisticated governmental and corporate equivalents have been responsible for the mid-twentieth-century "inflation."

The trouble with the Quantity Theory is that it doesn't take enough account of those mechanisms that we know to be the cause of rising prices in our time, including pushy businessmen, the self-aggrandizing worldwide military-industrial complex, bumptious union leaders, and greedy sheiks. Explanations that assign the blame for the rising cost of living to one or more of these villains lack the generality of the monetary approach; they fail to satisfy our most elementary sense of what constitutes an explanation. There were no "big unions" in the sixteenth century to account for "inflation" then. What is needed, then, is some more fundamental variable that can be used to explain both why prices are rising and why money is increasing to accommodate them.

Reporters rush in where scholars fear to tread. My interest in these topics grew out of three articles I wrote about the seven-hundred-year Phelps Brown price index for *Forbes* magazine in the mid-1970s. I wrote the first because I was asked to write on the likelihood that rising prices were coming to an end. I wrote the others because I had tumbled onto an anomaly in the usual explanations of the cost of living: the queer thing, I thought then, was that the level of prices in the twentieth century could be discussed without any consideration of the level of taxes. It seemed clear that taxes had gone up disproportionately, and that this increase in the cost of civilization obviously did affect the cost of living—not indirectly, through disincentive effects, but directly, as taxes entered into the cost of production. This was, of course, a primitive "tax-push" argument.

To suggest the mechanism at the heart of this process, I once quoted from the movie *Honky Tonk*, a 1941 Western in which Clark Gable plays a swindler-turned-sheriff who takes over a town. As he builds his gang—a "sector" that offers a new if unwelcome range of services to the town—the merchants complain about the cost. Gable murmurs to a henchman, "What do you mean, they can't pay more taxes? Tell 'em to put up the price of beans!" This process of cost "pushing"—the "diffusion of costs" is a better phrase—remains near the center of the analysis of this book, but it has taken all the years since then to learn to talk with greater clarity about that cinematic village, before and after Gable, and about the same processes as they work in the larger world. It required a very long journey of escape from the concept of a "relative price shift."

It turns out that it is enough to say that the economic world has become more complex. In a view of the economy in which changing complexity is the starting point, "inflation" isn't ultimately a monetary experience at all but rather a phenomenon that accompanies massive changes in the organization of work. It occurs when an economy becomes more complex, more variegated, and more interdependent, before it realizes the efficiencies of the new forms of organization it has adopted. There are extreme forms of rising prices, of course—the strato-inflations of Israel and Latin America and the hyperinflations of Shanghai and Weimar Germany—that seem to have little to do with growing complexity, but even in these situations it is possible to discover attempts to alter the underlying division of labor in the economy at the root. The purchasing power of money—as well as the quantity of money itself—depends upon the complexity of the system in which it is spent. Having begun by thinking about complexity as a way of talking about taxes and prices together, I slowly became aware of the community of students of complexity whose work is reported in these pages. At that point, this book ceased to be about "structural theories of inflation" and turned itself to the subject of economic complexity, with an emphasis on its applicability to the price level problem.

The argument here, then, is that these episodes of rising prices and increasing money that we call price explosions should be considered as the result of periods of "economic revolution," each exhibiting a relatively similiar structure to the others. In these revolutions, there is a great "front-ending" of costs as new patterns of the division of labor are created. New forms of financing economic expansion are devised. Prices rise. Eventually, economies of scope and scale take hold and the cost of living stabilizes at a new level. It makes sense to link the great cathedrals of the Middle Ages with the great hospitals of the modern era in this fashion, because each is a cause far more than an effect of the kind of explosive increase in the money supply that economists call "inflation."

Even without going into history, however, the significance of complexity for economic policy is no small matter. The fragility of an economic system, its ability to withstand economic shock, probably has a great deal to do with its complexity—an issue I discuss in Chapter 6. In Chapter 7 I offer a few very tentative conclusions about the implications of what has gone before. If the recognition of the effect of growing economic complexity on "inflation" were to shave just a point or two off the rate of increase of the consumer price index (a decidedly modest goal), the savings could amount to several tens of billions of dollars annually—the amount that wouldn't be passed through to workers in cost-of-living adjustments and wage hikes when CAT scanners are added to hospitals and killer satellites to the nuclear arsenal. Conversely, if an extra percentage point or two were added to the monetary growth targets to accommodate growth in economic complexity, similiar sums in extra gross national product might be obtained.* Trade agreements could be rewritten; regional and urban development plans would be redrawn.

The price-level implication of economic complexity is just one (and perhaps not the most important) of its ramifications. The fragility of the economy, the experience of living in it, the design of work itself, can each be understood better by thinking in terms of levels of complexity. When analysts debate the merits of "reindustrialization" and the perils of "deindustrialization," they are really talking about the consequences of increasing global economic complexity. It may be, as Robert Reich has written, that "the only way industrialized nations can increase their standards of living in the future is to concentrate on high-value niches within [mass-production] industries and to seize and keep world leadership in new industries based on advanced and emerging technologies." It may even be, as he says, that "this requires a different form of organization, one far more flexible and adaptable than the structures designed to support high-volume, standardized production." But until we develop tools for thinking about such complexity-related issues, we will be arguing in greater darkness than need be.

---

*The reader who says that I believe that the effects of technical and quality change are underestimated in the official indexes has misunderstood me. He is the same fellow who thinks that a city can be adequately described as a village with a great deal of technical change, that a fancy restaurant is simply a plain one with a lot of factor substitution. Although I'm sure that papers on "the economics of complexity" will begin to appear within a few years, I believe there is no way to go gracefully from one lens to the other; the approaches from equilibrium and from complexity are mutually exclusive.

THE IDEA OF
ECONOMIC COMPLEXITY

1

THE DISCOVERY OF COMPLEXITY

ON ANY PARTICULAR SUNDAY, *THE NEW YORK TIMES* USES THE words "complex" and "complexity" between twenty and forty times. Often it refers to nothing more forbidding than an "office complex" or a "shopping complex"; sometimes it turns up in the "Oedipus complex" or "a persecution complex." Usually it means "intricate," "thorny," or "complicated." We speak of complex corporations, complex symphonies, complex wines, complex moral problems, complex narratives, complex legal cases, and complex products as well as "the complexities of life." "There are no simple solutions to complex problems!" threatens to become the catchphrase of the '80s. The word is ubiquitous.

But does it mean anything? Of course it means "not simple," but aside from that, is it anything other than a dismissive adjective, used to mean "something you cannot understand or that I don't choose to explain"? Confronted by the drumbeat of everyday usage, one could be forgiven for lamenting, as one scholar of interdependence recently did, that the word "complexity" is nothing more than "the mirror image of confusion."

Yet far from following this common usage, the word "complexity" is coming to have an exact meaning in one field after another precisely because it *is* the mirror image of confusion. Measurable complexity is now used to describe biological systems, to crack codes, to design semiconductor chips, and to describe language. It is even banging its way into economics, via the back door. You might have thought that the existence of varying degrees of complexity would have been recognized and dealt with long ago, but the discovery of complexity is one of the major—if unheralded—scientific stories of our time.

TWO KINDS OF COMPLEXITY

A complex number is one that is part real and part imaginary —the square root of minus one divided by six, for example. A complex compound is one formed by simpler substances and held together by chemical (as opposed to physical) forces. But aside from "having more than one part," what does "complex" mean? A little bit more light, but not much, is shed on the problem by the wise lexicographer, who offers gradations of meaning. "Complex" means having interacting parts that require deep study of expert knowledge and refers to something that, at least in principle, can be mastered, such as the complex mechanism of a watch. "Complicated" means so complex as to be hard to understand or explain even for an expert, such as a complicated problem in mathematics. "Intricate" is just at or beyond whatever happens to be our current level of understanding, as in the intricate relationship between genetic material and culture and response. But nothing about the use of these words is written in stone: problems once thought impossibly intricate are now merely complex.

It is of no use to search the scientific encyclopedias and dictionaries for some concrete meaning to attach to complexity. *The Dictionary of the History of Science* notes that complexity of organization was invoked by late-eighteenth-century naturalists as a theoretical razor for distinguishing living from inanimate things, a distinction between simple and complex briefly succeeding the tripartite distinction between animal, vegetable, and mineral that dated back to Aristotle and beyond. But when a scheme based on increasing complexity of organization failed to produce a satisfactory scheme of biological classification for Jean Baptiste Lamarck, the idea was discarded.

When it comes to the Scientific Citation Index, however, we begin to turn up some results. Since 1965, more than 10,000 technical papers in the natural and behavioral sciences having the word "complexity" in their title have been published in English and recorded in this extensive index. The specialization and interdependence of everything from artichokes to yeasts has been investigated. Entries for combinatorial complexity, the complexity of algorithms, task complexity, stimulus complexity, and the measurement of complexity are among the most numerous (around a hundred papers each), but well over a thousand different categories are listed, and there are even a few papers on cost complexity to be found (though none on economic complexity). Complexity is an idea on the tip of the modern tongue.

The concept of complexity became an interesting topic only about the time of World War II. The era was one of those periodic "sea changes" that mark the history of science. Already in the 1930s and early 1940s Max Delbrück was writing about complexity in biology, Kurt Gödel in logic, and Alan Turing in mathematics. But it was war and its weapons that stimulated worldwide curiosity about the topic. John von Neumann began publishing on complexity after advancing the theory and development of computers in the course of his work on the atomic bomb. George Dantzig was working for the U.S. Air Force, Tjalling Koopmans on ship scheduling for the British, and Leonid V. Kanterovitch on the purest of mathematical problems in Leningrad before the war when they independently hit on the linear programming techniques that are now used to solve complex problems—and that won for Koopmans and Kanterovitch a Nobel Prize in economics. Phillip M. Morse and George Kimball, two American pioneers in the science of operations research, were writing on organized complexity in an explicit way by 1946. Warren McCullough and Walter Pitts were modeling the nervous system with automata theory at about the same time. Herbert Simon described the "architecture" of complexity in 1960, and in 1961 Friedrich von Hayek published on the theory of "complex systems." A number of more personal visions of complexity were enunciated in these years, including the General Systems Theory of Ludwig von Bertalanffy, and the Systems Dynamics of Jay W. Forrester at the Massachusetts Institute of Technology. So far, these groups have generally failed to link up with the mainstream of modern social science.

One of the first writers to discuss complexity as a measurable dimension was Warren Weaver, a mathematician who helped found modern information theory. In 1948 he offered a fundamental distinction between organized complexity and disorganized complexity that is still of great value.

Most of the problems that had been solved by science during its first three hundred years were relatively simple, "two-variable problems," says Weaver, in which one thing largely depends on another, and which submitted easily to the experiments and analysis of the scientific revolution. A good example, he says, was the law of gases, in which pressure depends mainly on volume in everyday life. Minor extensions of such laws to handle three or four variables—temperature and molecular weight, for example, in the case of the law of gases—were made over the years, and on the foundation of a few dozen such discoveries were erected the theories of light, sound, heat, and electricity—on which the entire edifice of the industrial age was built.

The problems that remained could be divided into two classes, writes Weaver. One of these was "disorganized complexity," which had to do with events arising from the interaction of very large numbers of variables. Such interactions nevertheless generated patterns that were generally predictable. Hundreds of billiard balls bouncing on a table, thousands of telephone calls coming to a switchboard, and the aging and death of large groups of people were all phenomena that could be handled by statistical techniques, "even though the individual event was as shrouded in mystery as is the chain of complicated and unpredictable events which leads to the accidental death of a healthy man."

"Organized complexity," on the other hand, had to do with the way in which complex systems such as living things were organized. How did DNA work? What caused cancer? Why could a salamander regenerate a leg whereas a man could not? These were problems that wouldn't submit to statistical methods, Weaver observes. Ultimately, a specific mechanism had to be discovered. It was to this class of problems that science would direct its focus for the next three hundred years.

In Weaver's opinion, most economic problems were problems of organized complexity. The price of wheat, the value of money, and the likelihood of depression were all "related in complicated but not in helter-skelter fashion." They required analysis as systems comprising organic wholes, all of whose parts existed in strong and intricate interrelationship. Clearly statistical techniques were not adequate for the analysis; it was necessary to know how the parts hung together.

In the Rockefeller Foundation report for 1958, Weaver—who was the director of its natural sciences program for thirty years—writes, "Indeed, if we only could, in the biological field, begin to learn how to deal with problems of organized complexity, then there might be opportunities to extend these new techniques, if only by helpful analogy, into vast areas of the behavioral and social sciences." How right he was!

LESSONS FROM ECOLOGY

The idea of complexity first began to gain widespread popular awareness through ecology. It is hard to remember a time when the intricate interconnectedness of nature was not well understood, but everyone has his favorite example of how someone, somewhere, learned this lesson.

One of the best such stories comes from Borneo. Some years ago, the World Health Organization undertook a DDT campaign there against malaria-carrying mosquitoes on behalf of the Dayak people. The DDT effectively killed the mosquitoes, but it also killed a parasitic wasp that controlled a thatch-eating caterpillar. It did not take long before Dayak roofs began collapsing. Worse, the cats of the region, which ate mosquito-eating lizards, died from the buildup of DDT in their bodies, and without the cats, jungle rats flourished, leading to an upsurge in cases of the plague. WHO resorted to parachuting cats into the jungle in an effort to reestablish the ecological balance.

At first glance the key seems to be equilibrium: out there in the jungle, everything is shifting, changing, balancing, counterbalancing, canceling out. Each species breeds in such a way as to increase its own level of population; those above it in the food chain hold it in check. Negative feedback is everything. The wonderful system of checks and balances that is nature's way obtains—unless disturbed by man.

But the idea of complexity should not be confused with the idea of equilibrium. Equilibrium has to do with the condition of balance that exists when opposing forces cancel each other out. A system of virtually any degree of complexity can be in equilibrium: a mere dozen species on a seashore in the Arctic, or of tens of thousands of species in a rain forest at the Equator. Complexity has to do with the number of different parts in an ecological system and how they interconnect.

Because there are many different parts, many different points of connection, many different things can go wrong in complex biological systems. Whether the number of parts and the intricacy of their connections have anything to do with the stability of the system is an open question. For a long time, researchers believed that complexity in a community of plants and animals was related to stability; the greater the number of types and the more tangled the web of relationships between species, and the stronger and more frequent the interactions between them, the less likely the system was thought to be affected by shocks, man-made or natural.

Then some theoretical ecologists produced mathematical models showing just the reverse: the greater the complexity, the more vulnerable the system was to perturbation, at least in theory. Remove a predator and the whole thing falls apart. Ever since, ecologists have been trying to puzzle it out—and have created clearer and clearer ideas of food web complexity as a result.

THE PRINCIPLE OF PLENITUDE

Interestingly, only in the last hundred and twenty-five years has it become possible to talk with real curiosity and significance about biological complexity. For most of recorded history, men believed that the species were a fixed inventory of types, unchanged since the day of their creation. This habit of thought—it boils down to the conviction that everything that can be created has been created—was characterized by Arthur O. Lovejoy as "the principle of plenitude." In a brilliant series of lectures published fifty years ago as *The Great Chain of Being,* he traced its roots back to Plato's myth of the creation, the *Timaeus.*

The assumption of plenitude was that the universe contains every conceivable kind of thing, that it was a *plenum formarum,* "in which the range of diversity of conceivable kinds of things is exhaustively exemplified," wrote Lovejoy. The vision of the world as being "complete once and for all and everlastingly the same in the kinds of its components" had its roots in the belief that God had done all He possibly could in creating the universe, for if He could have done more, He would have. It sounds strange to the modern ear, but for nearly two thousand years the principle of plenitude dominated man's conception of nature. It was central to many of the major battles of the scientific revolution.

For example, plenitude was invoked in the early debates about the nature of the atmosphere, to deny that vacuums were possible. How could there be a space that God hadn't filled with *something?* From the Copernican revolution, plenitude led immediately to the conclusion that there must be life on an infinity of other planets. In the early years of modern chemistry, it led scientists to imagine that all matter consisted of a few basic "principles" existing in an endless variety of combinations of varying proportions, rather than having been built up from the hundred or so basic building blocks we now know as elements. For a time, biologists argued against the modern interpretation of fossils on the ground that in a well-run universe, species couldn't be allowed to fail. With this, a certain kind of biology became a hunt for "missing links" in the great Chain of Being.

As it was disproven in particular respects, the axiom of plenitude fell back somewhat, from the assertion of the infinite static diversity of creation to the notion that plenitude entailed a process of gradually increasing diversificaton. No longer was the world simply the inventory that had been set out by the Creator but, rather, His ongoing program. The idea of evolution *toward* the state of plenitude took over from the idea of a continually existing state of fullness.

It is hard now to imagine what was necessary for a belief in plenitude. Recall the title of Charles Darwin's seminal book: *On the Origin of Species*. In the early nineteenth century, that title to most everybody but a scientist would have sounded odd, even blasphemous. The critical ear would have thought that it should have included another definite article, that it should have been *On the Origin of the Species*. After all, *the* species were those God had created, those Noah had saved.

I mention all of this because plenitude is, in its way, as much an antonym of complexity as is "simplicity" or "disorganization." The point is that if the world is plenitudinous, it has an unchanging degree of complexity. (As Leibniz put it, "In every particle of the universe a world composed of an infinity of creatures is contained.") The idea of "development" has no place in this scheme of things. The degree of "many-partedness" of the overall system is nearly meaningless in a world with an unchanging variety of parts.

Among other things, a belief in the plenitude of the world makes comparisons in time quite easy: you can speak about the number of frogs in 80,000 B.C. against the number of frogs today, for example, with no need to specify when the first frog of the sort you are talking about made its appearance.

Indeed, from a scientific standpoint, time ceases to be very interesting at all if continuous change is a necessity, with no sudden jumps from one sort of thing to another. In a plenitudinous world, the problem remains of whether a frog is more complex than an orange, or whether equatorial communities are more complex than Arctic communities, but it is a much less interesting question. Metaphorically, complexity goes nowhere if the degree of diversity in the world is a constant. The haunting question "Is life getting more complex, and if so how?" is answered simply. The more things change, the more they remain the same.

The notion that things today are pretty much as they have always been, that there is nothing new under the sun, is deeply embedded in our political and economic thought. In the seventeenth century, for example, it required a bitter battle for Sir Henry Spelman to demonstrate that there had ever been a time in which the English Parliament did not exist. (He was trying to establish that the king had the right to send Parliament home.) The result of his research was the discovery of feudalism—and a powerful new lens for looking at the past.

COMPUTERS AND COMPLEXITY

If even a cursory understanding of biological systems requires the idea of complexity, there is a man-made creation even more demanding of the concept—the computer.

The saga of modern information theory has been told quite

wonderfully by Jeremy Campbell in his book *Grammatical Man*. He opens up the topics of cybernetics and linguistics with grace and punch ("Wiener would walk into Fano's room, puffing at a cigar and say, 'Information is entropy.' Then he would turn around and walk out again without another word. . . ."), observing in the process that the point of much of what has been learned is that "the world need not regress towards the simple, the uniform and the banal, but may advance in the direction of richer and more complex structures, physical and mental." Information theory, Campbell says, suggests that systems of all kind "evolve towards more complex states, and . . . this is the natural order of things. We should not expect them to behave in any other way."

A major figure in the early study of complexity was Alan Turing, a British mathematician who achieved a memorable formulation of the problem of complexity when in 1936 he imagined a machine—now called a Turing machine—that would read an endless tape, compute numbers on the basis of a few simple instructions, and stop when it achieved an answer (or eventually break if there was no answer). Another pioneer was the great Hungarian mathematician and physicist John von Neumann, who called his work on complexity "automata" theory. He reasoned that what was necessary was to think of complex phenomena as consisting of various machines of particular sorts. (Those funny black boxes that, on the flip of a switch, produce a hand to turn themselves off are automata. Automata have a long history reaching back to China during the Han Dynasty, forward to a few delightful machines produced by Carl Fabergé.) But the rather forbidding word "automata" masked a wide array of applications: automata theory is the basis for discussing complex systems from language to biological reproduction.

Part of the key to understanding complexity is the idea of redundancy. Von Neumann reasoned that redundancy was a complex system's way of dealing with failure. Failure was a completely natural (if undesirable) part of complex systems, and the more complex a system, the more likely that one or more of its parts would not work. (Enrico Fermi, the physicist, had predicted that the first computer, a room full of vacuum tubes, would run for less than five minutes without breaking down; in fact, it ran for several hours before stopping.) As surely as redundancy had to be built into machines, von Neumann writes, it had to be built into language itself: "Redundancy is the only thing which makes it possible to write a text which is longer than, say, ten pages. In other words, a language that has maximum compression would actually be completely unsuited to conveying information beyond a certain degree of complexity, because you could never find out whether a text is right or wrong. It follows, therefore, that the complexity of the medium in which you work has something to do with redundancy."

Another key here is hierarchy. Herbert Simon pointed out years ago, in an interesting essay on the architecture of complexity, that evolution favors the hierarchically organized. He asks his readers to imagine two watchmakers assembling watches consisting of ten thousand parts. He asks them further to suppose that the watchmakers were constantly interrupted by telephone calls and that to put a partially completed watch down would be to have it fall apart.

The watchmaker who designed his watches in such a way that each was composed of ten stable subassemblies of a thousand parts each, which in turn were composed of ten subassemblies of a hundred parts, which in turn were composed of ten subassemblies of ten parts, would have a very great advantage over the watchmaker who started from scratch each time. Such hierarchy was almost always encountered in complexity in nature, Simon writes.

According to Simon, hierarchy leads to redundancy and redundancy to the decomposability of hierarchically organized units—which offers the hope that complexity can be fairly simply described. He went on to apply the concept of hierarchy to human problem-solving and to artificial intelligence—and to win a Nobel Prize for his work in economics in the process.

A CERTAIN URGENCY

Meanwhile, the project of learning to describe and measure complexity has been taken up by an increasing number of hands, largely because it is becoming a significant factor in everyday problems. A central practical problem has been amassing information and getting access to it quickly and efficiently. Elegant architecture is crucial to the ability of computers to perform complex calculations in reasonable amounts of time.

For example, take very large-scale circuit integration, which the semiconductor industry is said to regard as its number one problem. According to Arthur L. Robinson, a reporter for *Science*, the key question here is how to bring the complexity of chip design down to a level at which it can be managed. "There are few systems in the world, electronic or otherwise, that consist of a million or more parts," he writes. "Organizing a million transistors on a silicon chip into a useful circuit is a formidable undertaking, and the tools for designing such a complex device do not yet exist."

Typical of the first tentative steps toward a solution, according to Robinson, is a technique developed at the California Institute of Technology in which a computer program called "bristle blocks," which designs circuits that can be joined together like the children's toy, can do in a few minutes what would otherwise take three man-years. There are other such techniques, and more are developed every day. Indeed, respected computer scientists have ventured that there is reason to believe that the integrated circuit revolution has run only half its course; "the change in complexity of four or five orders of magnitude that has taken place during the last fifteen years appears to be only the first half of a potentially eight-order-of-magnitude development" of integrated circuits, according to a paper published by I. E. Sutherland, Carver A. Mead, and T. E. Everhart.

What is true of hardware is also true of software, the vast array of systems that are designed to tailor computers to particular tasks. Software engineering developed swiftly: as a great body of techniques came into being with no theoretical underpinning, the field "leapfrogged its scientific foundations," as researchers put it. "Computer science does not suffer from a lack of proposed metrics," according to Marvin Denicoff and Robert Grafton, who have organized research in the field. They add, however, that "many are being used out of necessity without the benefit of a deep understanding." An effort to catch up is therefore afoot in big computer laboratories around the world. "Software metrics" is a lively field, no more than a few years old, designed to produce suitable yardsticks for talking about key questions in software design. How much memory does a system require? How much speed? How much will it cost? How long will it take to create? When will it have to be replaced? What will it take to make it better? Attempts to answer these questions are known as "complexity studies."

The effort to describe and measure complexity is also being driven forward by the need to protect coded information. Indeed, the possibilities for code cracking that are offered by powerful computers are spawning the development of a new branch of mathematics called complexity theory. The central problem here concerns the description of what makes a calculation difficult instead of easy, complex as opposed to simple. What distinguishes the sort of operation that takes a computer hours to perform? And, more important, what distinguishes the sort of computation that even a powerful computer might never have time to complete? On such questions hang very weighty matters, including the cracking of military codes.

These things needn't concern us in any detail. They do suggest that metrics for complexity are not very far away—and that however rigorously grounded in deep theory they may be, they won't be very different on the surface from the rule-of-thumb metrics we now use to distinguish between levels of computational complexity when we speak of tasks suitable for microcomputers, minicomputers, mainframes, and supercomputers. And they also suggest that the concepts of information and hierarchy are central to the business of understanding complexity.

THE LAW AGAINST COMPLEXITY

Meanwhile, quite far from these practical, even urgent pursuits, there is the extension of abstract theorizing about complexity to the most basic notions through which we understand the world. Today, the universality of even the most fundamental tendency known to man—the tendency of systems to consume more energy than they produce—is open to doubt.

Recall the celebrated Second Law of Thermodynamics, as formulated by the nineteenth-century German physicist Rudolf Clausius, familiarly rendered as "the universe is running down." In the Second Law, the physical systems of the universe are seen to be progressing irrevocably in the direction of disorganization, toward "the death of heat." Entropy, the measure of this disorganization, is forever increasing. This idea, much beloved as a metaphor, has been cited by people as diverse as Henry Adams, Arthur Eddington, Barry Commoner, and Thomas Pynchon. It amounts to a law against growing complexity.

It is true that there is an everyday, observable tendency of life and human effort to achieve ever-greater degrees of complexity, but such big puzzles are not the stuff of which successful scientific problems are made. Science thrives by asking smaller and smaller questions until it finds one it can answer. Living things were granted an exemption from the Second Law as representing a statistical aberration and were not very closely examined. The problem of how complexity arises in the physical world began to receive widespread attention from physicists only after the Russian chemist B. P. Belousov published a report in an obscure journal of radiation medicine about a certain strange chemical reaction.

It had been noticed, Belousov wrote in 1958, that if citric

acid and sulfuric acid were dissolved in water with potassium bromate and a cerium salt, the result was a mixture that changed color periodically from colorless to pale yellow and then back again. This "oscillator" was, in effect, a "chemical clock," operating in what seemed to be clear violation of the Second Law of Thermodynamics, which dictates that reactions are supposed to go straight to equilibrium and stay there. "If A goes to B, it must do so throughout the reaction without detours back to A along the way" is the way Irving Epstein, a distinguished chemist, has put it, describing Belousov's discovery.

Today, there is a large catalogue of simple physical phenomena that appear to contradict the Second Law. Precipitates of certain chemical reactions flash in bands instead of uniformly diffusing; cellular structures appear in fluids heated to a certain point, as if by magic. And these are just the very simplest reactions to exhibit what must be called a metabolism, a process in which new material is assimilated to repair the waste. They offer only dim hints of the astonishing variety of life, which has been advancing in the direction of ever greater diversity and complexity for millennia. Why has order emerged from chaos if chaos is forever supposed to be increasing? How do we square this apparent "building up" of evolution with the "winding down" rule of the Second Law?

No scientist has been more instrumental in revising the way we think of the physical basis for complexity than a Belgian chemist named Ilya Prigogine, who won the Nobel Prize in chemistry in 1977. Prigogine's "theory of non-dissipative structures" is a kind of rump thermodynamics, for it suggests ways in which spontaneous organization can take place. According to Itamar Proccacia and John Ross, who wrote of the award for *Science*, Prigogine and his colleagues achieved results that require only one thermodynamic law but that acknowledge two different states: near equilibrium and far from it. Prigogine found that feedback loops would drive reactions far from equilibrium; there the system would become unstable and evolve spontaneously to new structures with different behavior. In this way he explained the behavior of Belousov's "chemical clock" —and a great many similar reactions too.

Prigogine likens these systems to a town, which can exist only as long as food and fuel come in while products and wastes flow out, and Irving Epstein, a distinguished chemist writing with tongue only partly in cheek, says that "living systems are the most interesting and varied examples of open, far-from-equilibrium oscillators. They are maintained in a non-equilibrium state by the input of reactants (nutrients) from the external environment and the output of products (wastes). If either of these fluxes is stopped, the organism and its oscillations must die."

The conclusions Prigogine draws from his work tend to be fairly sweeping and enthusiastic. For example, in *From Being to Becoming: Time and Complexity in the Physical Sciences,* he says that coming to grips with complexity entails a revision for physical science as fundamental as the original formulation of the scientific approach in ancient Greece or its renaissance in the time of Galileo. Others are even more enthusiastic about the implications they see in Prigogine's work. In *The Self-Organizing Universe,* Erich Jantsch, a lecturer at the Center for Research in Management at the University of California at Berkeley, offers "a new world view" based on Prigogine's work. He says it "emphasizes process over structure, no equilibrium over equilibrium, evolution over permanency and individual creativity over collective stabilization." "An age-old vision is finding its scientific foundations," he says before launching into "a synopsis of the three major phases of the co-evolution of macro- and microcosmos—cosmic, chemical/biological/sociobiological/ecological and sociocultural evolution."

For the record, I am inclined to believe that we are on the verge of a fairly sweeping transformation of the way in which processes of change in time are seen, though I balk at calling it "the Aquarian Conspiracy," as the writer Marilyn Ferguson has suggested.

A SUPERSATURATED SOLUTION

Naturally, the social sciences have not been altogether oblivious to the idea of measurable complexity. But either the concept is examined at a relatively informal level, as in Marvin Harris's book *America Now*, or else it develops as rather far afield from what is meant in this book by "economic complexity" in the division of labor. Professor Harris writes, "The growth of the service and information economy and of giant government and corporate oligopolies has had a far more pervasive effect on American life than most people realize." And to be sure, he is right as far as he goes, which is pretty far. He says that growing complexity explains "why nothing works, why the help won't help you, why the dollar shrank, why women left home, why the gays came out of the closet, why there's terror on the streets, why the cults are coming, [and] why America changed." Harris's analysis, shrewd as it is, is somewhat vague, but his personal response has been downright concrete: he left New York City for Florida.

Linguists, anthropologists, and mathematical sociologists all have their own ideas about the importance of complexity. Linguists, led by Noam Chomsky, have gone perhaps the furthest in developing the concept of complexity in examining the structures of language, but controversies are budding in anthropology, where the concept is used as a basis for the comparison of cultures. Not surprisingly, there is a deep emotional divide in such questions: between those interested in establishing a continuum between "primitive" and "highly developed" cultures and those who think such comparisons serve no useful purpose except to denigrate those cultures that do not share Western values. Economists have been the social scientists least interested in complexity, perhaps because they believe the whole point of their method is to permit them to penetrate the superficial complexity of events.

Yet it is precisely in economics that a formal concept of complexity promises the greatest gains in understanding. It is economics, perhaps alone among the modern sciences, that still deals with a plenitudinous world and that has failed to recognize the importance of development and the significance of historical time to its subject matter. Ask an economist about the difference between the economic systems in 1520 and in 1980, and the best he can offer is an estimate of the difference in the per capita income of a European peasant and a suburban office worker. Ask him the difference between New York City and Poona, India, and he'll tell you New York has a bigger production function. The mind-boggling differences in the degree of specialization and interdependence of the respective economic systems go entirely unremarked. It will take the notion of variations in the degree of complexity, or something very much like it, to augment this approach in the realms where it is least useful.

I've sketched a picture of a movement going forward in science along a broad front. It may seem unnecessarily far from our central concerns, which are, after all, with economics and understanding the history of specialization. I have dwelt on it at chapter length, however, in order to explain that economic complexity is a concept with certain antecedents and analogues in other disciplines; it is one of those ideas that can seem entirely peripheral one day—and be absolutely central the next. In the historian Stephen Toulmin's telling metaphor of a similar, earlier transformation of point of view, the situation in social science today resembles a supersaturated solution that keeps its homogeneity and liquidity only precariously: "A few small crystals dropped into the solution—and the transformation is at once precipitated."

2

THE IDEA OF ECONOMIC COMPLEXITY

NO ONE WHO HAS LIVED THROUGH EVEN A FEW DECADES OF THE twentieth century can doubt that complexity and economic interdependence have been growing at a remarkable rate. When the century began, people traveled by horse and rail and communicated by mail, a third of the population lived and worked on farms, and a specialist was a cavalry lieutenant or an organic chemist. Children were born at home and old people died there. A few industries were organized in great trusts—gunpowder, sugar, shoes, tobacco, oil, and some others—but compared with today's vertical integration, these were simple operations, run out of their founders' vest pockets. The government in Washington, D.C., employed a few thousand people organized in two dozen offices. As late as the 1920s, the Senate met for only three months a year.

Today, soldiers operate nuclear missiles and submarines, businesses are managed by experts in long hierarchical chains, and even physicists work in teams. Three percent of the work force now does the farming; the rest engage in a bewildering array of manufacturing and services. The telephone and the television have replaced the postal service and the Saturday night dance. Products have proliferated almost beyond the naming of them; indeed, technical writers capable of clearly describing the differences between products and their functions are in great demand. There are plastics manufacturers, television producers, nuclear weapons specialists, molecular biologists, strategic planners, fast-food hamburger cooks, astronauts, foreign currency traders, CAT-scan operators, Social Security actuaries, chip designers, corporate takeover specialists, Xerox repairmen, Occupational Health and Safety Administration inspectors, and historians of science—all of them specialists, none of whose jobs existed in any significant numbers before World War II.

Moreover, there has been a dramatic increase in international specialization. Pins now come from Poland, automobiles from Japan, fish from Argentina, televisions from Taiwan, and oil—as everybody knows—from Arabia, Nigeria, and Mexico. You can buy Pepsi-Cola in Siberia, Revlon cosmetics in Argentina, Nestlé's baby formula in Bali, and Kirin beer in Chicago. The financial structure has become global as well. Banks are widely diversified in their lending; now the pension funds and mutual funds are diversifying internationally, adding the securities of European and Asian firms to their portfolios. The same process of integration into a larger and more complex economy that began assimilating the "island communities" of American cities and towns into the national economy at the end of the last century has now been extended to the nations of the world. The same benefits of membership in a larger market that eighty years ago were conferred upon Pittsburgh and Moline are today being gained in Brazil and Korea: more jobs in specialized industries and higher standards of living. The same costs to the community are being exacted by the process of integration, too: the loss of undifferentiated jobs and, for many, a loss of meaning, as jobs once thought vitally important are "exported" to some faraway place.

This process of increasing global specialization and integration is surely the most striking social development of our time.

Observers have resorted to phrases as various as "the new industrial revolution," "the great transformation," "the managerial revolution," "the post-industrial society," "the age of organization," and even "the third wave" to describe it.

Yet when we pass to the scholarly disciplines from which most of our picture of the social world is derived, there is very little help to be had in understanding economic differentiation. There is no convenient way of talking about it. It is easy enough to understand why we gloss over changing complexity in everyday life: we value continuity of experience and resist the implication that our lives are, in any important way, different from those of our parents and grandparents. It is harder to explain the absence of any formal notion of complexity in the social sciences. In fact, in modern technical economics, where you would expect the concept of complexity to be most fully developed, it isn't found at all.

THE IDEA THAT ISN'T THERE

How do economists deal with problems of what they call "structure"? The best answer is, gingerly.

In a broad, descriptive way, "development" comes close to what we mean by increasing complexity, but the term is exceedingly hazy. So are "urbanization" and "modernization." The words commonly employed to discuss these matters, "structure" and "institutions"—as in "There has been a lot of structural or institutional change"—are even worse. "Infrastructure" captures part of the meaning of economic complexity, but only part.

There are phrases such as "technical change" and "technological change," the headings under which many of the topics connected with increasing specialization are most frequently discussed, but, for the most part, economists prefer to focus on the inventions themselves rather than on the patterns of employment they generate. As a result, one can read an entire book, like Nathan Rosenberg's excellent survey, *Inside the*

Black Box: Technology and Economics, and get no feeling at all for the increasing specialization of the world. Modernity? Just a lot of technical change. Nowhere in the book is there a breakdown of employment by specialties. Rosenberg defines technology in terms of its effect on output, meaning that it is whatever gets you more bang for the buck. That is very interesting in some connections, but it is not very helpful when it comes to describing the networks of specialists that grow up around various kinds of knowledge and manufacturing processes.

Colin Clark's distinction among the primary, secondary, and tertiary sectors of an economy is a very useful contribution to the concept of complexity, but it doesn't go nearly far enough; and other disaggregating terms like "infrastructure" and "intermediate goods" are trivial building blocks. There is the Austrian notion of "roundaboutness," meaning the number of steps that are gone through in the production process. But one would feel silly talking about the "growing roundaboutness of the world," even if we could agree on what was meant. And John Hicks's term for the economic effects of particular technological advances—the Impulse—seems only a little more promising.

Interesting terms like "taste change" and "changing preferences," concepts that fall within the province of the theory of consumer demand, usually permit changing complexity to be factored out of economists' equations, to be treated as so much noise. "Assume stable preferences" means that when it comes to measuring their satisfaction, people are really buying the same old things, whether their need for transportation takes the form of oxcarts or sports cars. Economic complexity disappears.

The concept of externalities, meaning the costs on others imposed beyond the immediate environs of the price system, offers a tantalizing glimpse of complexity but nothing more. The insurance premiums that others must pay because of bad drivers and the cleaning bills homeowners pay in the vicinity of a coal-fired electricity plant are externalities, but they don't help us very much at all in gaining an overall picture of the complexity of a system.

Certainly the idea of economic growth doesn't come close to what is meant by complexity; growth has to do with the money value of what is produced, and it is traditionally measured in terms of gross national product per citizen—so much per person in New York, so much per person in Dubuque—whereas complexity is something that obviously cannot be measured with money. Nor do any of the other familiar macroeconomic variables—the consumer price index (CPI), the unemployment rate, the rate of productivity gain—tell us much worth knowing about complexity. To judge from what economists have to say about the performance of the economy, any change in the degree of complexity since 1939 is purely coincidental; the "production function"—meaning our ability to turn "inputs" into "outputs"—is a little greater, that's all. All one needs to know about the modern world is that gross national product per capita has grown dramatically, says the economist; never mind the burst of specialization that has taken place.

Indeed, the most interesting writing about complexity has come from far outside economics. Architecture generally has produced much of it; Robert Venturi's book *Complexity and Contradiction in Architecture* is a landmark. But more than any other, it is Jane Jacobs who has illuminated issues of economic complexity in a graceful and penetrating way over a long career. In her first book, *The Death and Life of Great American Cities,* she took on a generation of architects and city planners in arguing that diversity and close interconnection were what caused a city's growth; planners should permit urban vitality to burst forth "from the bottom up" rather than seek to impose sterile order on the metropolis from above. In *The Economy of Cities,* she argued that cities—"problems in organized complexity" she called them—were the engines of economic development. And in her most recent book, *Cities and the Wealth of Nations: Principles of Economic Life,* Jacobs explores, among many other topics, the role of currency exchange rates as feedback control mechanisms that convey important information about cities' export trade positions. Attention to the range of interactions in cities, the diversity of skills and products, and the dominating metabolism of export and import are characteristic of Jacobs's vivid approach.

A SHORT HISTORY OF TALK
ABOUT THE DIVISION OF LABOR

Complexity has to do with the extent of the division of labor —with the *overall* division of labor, in the provision not of just one product or service but of all products and services taken together, for the contention here is that the division of labor concerns the proliferation of tasks as well as their subdivision. The phrase thus connotes a far wider world than is usually envisioned.

We talk about the complexity of an economy rather than its "diversity" because we assume from long experience that the parts of an economy make up an interdependent whole. We don't speak of the degree of "diversity" of a watch with many moving parts, for example, because it is understood that all the watch parts fit together to form a single machine. For the same reason we speak of the "complexity" rather than the "diversity" of an economy; we assume it is an integrated whole, a semiclosed system. For similar reasons, we say "complexity" rather than "structure," because to speak of the "structure" of something—of a watch, of a society—is to suggest a property that is unique, a dimension that does not often alter its configuration. You can't say of the world that its "structure" has grown. It may very well be that what we call structural change is "difficult," meaning that it happens only when all of the adaptive energies of a system have been exhausted, but that is not the same as saying that only a few different degrees of complexity exist, sharply isolated from one another. Cities come in all different kinds of economic structures, for example, but presumably their complexity can be measured on a more or less continuous scale. Who doesn't possess some intuitive gauge of the differing complexity of villages, towns, and cities?

What, precisely, are the "parts" that a complex economy comprises? They are jobs—different kinds of jobs. We might call them economic niches. There are many different ways of aggregating them: the distinction between blue collar and white collar, for example, or between proletariat and bourgeoisie. Nowadays we talk most frequently about the "sectors" of an economy: an economy with a service sector is probably more complex than one without; an economy with a highly developed military-industrial establishment is probably more complex than the economy of a pacifist nation.

Note that there are several aspects of economic complexity—parameters, an economist would say. They have to do with the way the parts of the economy connect, with the degree of their interdependence, as well as the degree of specialization. Is the economy highly decentralized or tightly controlled? Is there a great deal of interaction between its components or are transactions done only rarely? Is there a great range to transactions? Or are they mostly local? Are the connections between economic agents intricate, based on social relationships, or are they strictly a matter of cash? What about the complexity of the individual unit? Are consumers a force in the economy? A theoretical lens of higher resolution will be needed before these concepts can be handled with any precision, but just because there is no simple measurement of complexity to be taken is no reason to despair. Even physicists have had to learn to live with a host of attributes (the "spin," "charm," and "strangeness," for example) of their subatomic particles. The complexity of an economy is an objective, measurable dimension. It is just that measuring it won't be easy.

Why is economic complexity such an inaccessible topic? The real reason for its not being a familiar analytic category has to do with the history of the debate over the division of labor. Such a debate starts with Plato, who took much the same attitude as John Kenneth Galbraith toward the division of labor—

some specialization was all right, but in his own day it had gone too far.

For a long time thereafter, the overall division of labor was dealt with simply. Some of the classic representations of the subject are still familiar. St. Paul explained that the working world is like the body of Christ: some men performed the role of the brain, others were as the hands and feet. That conceit changed, and European society of the Middle Ages knew itself to have only three sectors: men farmed or fought or prayed. There was considerable intellectual heat beginning in the late Middle Ages, when a "fourth estate" was discovered to have been established. Thereupon a story of the "four stages" of man took hold: hunting, pasturage, agriculture, and commerce.

By the early eighteenth century, the division of labor had progressed so far as to be a familiar topic of conversation. In 1705, Bernard Mandeville published *The Grumbling Hive*, a work subsequently retitled *The Fable of the Bees* and subtitled *Private Vices, Public Benefits*. This long poem rejoiced in the division of labor, celebrated spending, denigrated saving. Then, however, the subject was taken over by Adam Smith.

THE DISCOVERY OF FEEDBACK

Adam Smith was a Scot, a friend of Sir James Hutton and of David Hume. He was a teacher, a lecturer, an admirer of scientists, and a man who traveled widely in England and Europe. His book *Inquiry into the Nature and Causes of the Wealth of Nations*, published in 1776, became a considerable best-seller. It also became the cornerstone of economics. Before Adam Smith, there were any number of writers on money; afterward, there was political economy.

In the first two luminous chapters of *The Wealth of Nations*, Smith lays out virtually all that is familiar today about the concept of the division of labor. Specialization had three advantages, he notes: it cut the time involved in production, improved skill, and permitted machines to enter the process. It arose from "the propensity to truck, barter and exchange one thing for another." It permitted men to pursue their natural talent. The result was social interdependence—and national wealth.

"Observe the accommodation of the most common artificer or day-laborer in a civilized and thriving country, and you will perceive that the number of people of whose industry a part, though but a small part, has been employed in procuring him this accommodation, exceeds all computation." The wool coat alone, says Smith, required the coordinated efforts of the shepherd, the sorter, the carder, the dyer, the scribbler, the weaver, the fuller, and the dresser. Then you had to add in the sailors who brought the coat to market, and the ropemakers, sailcutters, and ironmongers who supplied them, and the brokers and merchants and bankers who maintained the retail apparatus. "If we examine, I say, all these things, and consider what a variety of labor is employed about each of them, we shall be sensible, that without the assistance and cooperation of many thousands, the very meanest in a civilized country could not be provided . . . the easy and simple manner in which he is commonly accommodated."

In the third chapter of his book, however, Smith's argument took a highly significant turn. He says that "the division of labor is limited by the extent of the market." A porter can't make a living in a small town, for example; people carry their own bags, so there is not enough demand for the porter's services. To make his way, a porter needs a big city. The size of a market also depends on the transportation available; a day's travel on bad roads can double the price of a basket of corn, whereas water transport costs far less. "What goods could bear the expense of land carriage between London and Calcutta?" Smith wonders. Soon thereafter, Smith launches into a discussion of the determination of price by markets.

So what is a market? It is a place where people gather to buy and sell. Originally it was a physical place, a square in the center of town where farmers, merchants, and craftsmen brought their goods for display. But the word has been generalized to mean any community of persons who carry on extensive transactions in any commodity. A market might be physically located in one place, such as the oil market in Rotterdam, the stock markets in New York City, or the gold markets in Zurich and London, and yet be composed of traders all over the world. There are presumably as many different kinds of markets as there are different kinds of goods.

What a market does, of course, is regulate production by adjusting the prices and quantities, for what is a price but a certain kind of very concrete information? English economists would make much of the threefold law of supply and demand that underlies the adjustments that constitute the workings of any market. When, they would say, at a particular price, demand exceeds supply, price tends to rise; when supply exceeds demand, price tends to fall. A rise in prices tends to cut demand and to increase supply, and a fall in price tends to increase demand and cut supply. Finally, price tends toward the level at which demand is equal to supply—in other words, toward an equilibrium. The better the communication, the more nearly perfect a market is. The more rapidly the information passes between buyers and sellers, the stronger the tendency for the same price to be paid for the same thing throughout the market.

In some ways, this is the beginning and end of economics. The number and kinds of markets have increased considerably since Adam Smith's time. The computer and the telephone have replaced the post office and the auction pit. But markets are still the heart of the matter, and the buyer side and the seller side are the only things that count. Today in London there are markets for petroleum, semiconductors, uranium, light bulbs, and countless other products, each serving as a kind of control center for a complicated, often worldwide network of jobs involved in the production of the item being traded. This vision of interrelated markets—along with the assumption that everyone in the world has a certain shopping list in mind, and that they are forever making nice calculations about the circumstances in which they would do with a little less of one thing in order to get a little more of some other—offers a way of thinking of the economic world as an immense system in which everything is related in price and quantity to everything else through what economists like to call "the calculus of human choice."

But are specialization and markets really so intimately connected, as Adam Smith supposed, that we may study the one and forget the other? I don't think so. For one thing, much of the specialization that exists in the world has little or nothing to do with buying and selling, as understood in any conventional sense.

THINKING ABOUT SPECIALIZATION

There are two problems with the economists' approach to specialization. The first is that the market approach is only one of two broad ways to achieve the division of labor. Politics is the other. Standing on the bridge of an aircraft carrier during flight operations is strangely similar to standing in the gallery of a grain exchange in the Midwest during trading hours. Down below, men in different-colored coats pursue a great variety of different kinds of jobs; that is, they participate in intricate divisions of labor. But whereas the trading pit is the very apotheosis of "capitalism," the carrier deck is a thoroughly "planned" or "command" economy. Smith dealt with this problem by sweeping it under the rug. Police, judges, kings, and soldiers—each a specialist of a sort, none really a creature of the market, all well known to Smith—were all consigned to the back of *The Wealth of Nations*. Economists have since learned to talk about "the demands for kings," "the supply of knowledge," and "the price of work" (which is forgone leisure), and "the demand for children" as if there were a shadowy market in which these things were determined, and in a sense there is. People do, after all, make these choices. But the rigid distinction between "prices," which support private divisions of labor (or "patterns of specialization," if you prefer), and taxes, which support public divisions of labor, is highly suspicious in a science that prides itself on clarity.

As soon as we make specialization rather than markets our focus, a second, more serious problem arises: there are at least two distinctly different kinds of division of labor, and there may be others. One involves learning to make the same old product more cheaply through the subdivision of tasks. The other involves making new and different products. I propose to call the result of these two kinds of the division of labor Type A complexity (subdivision of tasks) and Type B complexity (product differentiation).

(Sociologists describe the subdivision of tasks as "routinization," and the creation of new jobs as "specialization"; they have learned to measure the extent of the division of labor with tools like the Gibbs-Martin index. Gerhard Lenski has even distinguished between societies on the basis of their "structural complexity"—meaning the extent of the division of labor, the degree of stratification, and the amount of inequality. But so far, sociologists have not sought to tie the two kinds of division of labor together, nor to investigate their macroeconomic significance.)

Type A complexity, the result of routinization, is the more familiar. It is associated with assembly-line or mass-production styles of organization. Often these styles of production use machines, have standardized work rules, and involve centralized purchasing. They always involve long production runs, making hundreds and perhaps millions of the same item. Pin manufacture is a famous example; Adam Smith began *The Wealth of Nations* with a recitation of the efficiencies of a pin factory. ("One man draws out the wire, another straightens it, a third cuts it, a fourth points it, a fifth grinds it at the top for receiving the head. . . .")

In Type B complexity, the kinds of goods and services of-

fered for sale proliferate. Nicely differentiated substitutes arise
to be preferred for one reason or another. Instead of making the
same old thing, workers make new and often more complex
products. Now the specialization occurs in the manufacture of
staples, zippers, or Velcro fasteners. The advent of these products and their manufacturing processes contributes to increased
economic specialization in the world beyond the pin factory.
They often require new forms of education and training. This is
the division of labor in its broad and significant sense, the one
that permits us to talk about its complexity and interdependence. The degree of specialization in the modern pin factory is
greater today than ever: one man keeps the books, another is
personnel manager, a third searches out foreign markets, a
fourth repairs the Xerox machine, and so forth.

The fact is that "the division of labor" is a portmanteau
term; it means two different things at once. The ambiguity entailed by these two kinds of complexity is reflected in the different connotations of "he's a specialist" (and therefore expensive)
or "it's assembly line" (and therefore cheap). Volume and experience may indeed bring unit costs down; think of telephone
calls, or computation time, or of how, in the early years of this
century, the price of a Model T dropped from more than
$1,000 to $315 as the number of cars sold soared. But often
these prices don't fall very far. There is no such thing as a $2
car, for example. Interestingly, the money price and the actual
cost of a product sometimes can go in opposite directions as we
learn to make products we've never made before; that is, money
prices often climb while actual cost is falling. Cars are a good
example: in terms of the labor it takes to buy one, the cost of
a new car has been dropping even while its money price has
risen.

In economics, these arguments about the effect on costs of
the division of labor are usually made in terms of increasing and
decreasing returns to scale, or whether long-run average costs
climb or fall when production of particular goods such as cars

or hamburgers is increased. Most economists believe that decreasing returns and higher long-run costs predominate; the land goes fallow, the mine plays out, the machine breaks down, the worker tires, and the profit to be had from each succeeding sale ultimately declines. This belief is one reason that economics is called "the dismal science." In a celebrated paper of 1928, however, the English economist Allyn Young argues that his science had got it backward. Because of the broadening of the market that occurs with increasing production, and because the division of labor occurs in all industries rather than just in the one observed, increasing returns were the rule rather than the exception, reasons Young. "The mechanism of increasing returns is not to be discerned adequately by observing the effects of the size of the individual firm or of a particular industry. . . . What is required is that industrial operations be seen as an interrelated whole." What was important, he said, was that the economy was constantly changing: "The counterforces which are continually defeating the forces which make for equilibrium are more pervasive and more deeply rooted than we commonly realize."

The debate about economies of scale and scope is still a lively topic in economics. Allyn Young, like Joseph Schumpeter, was a "supply-sider," locating in the businessman's entrepreneurial search for markets the most profound impulse toward economic growth. We are coming at it from a slightly different direction in this book, that is all. Instead of seeking to puzzle out the mechanism of an assumed general economic equilibrium, we are simply looking for a relationship between degrees of complexity and the quantity of money. In Chapters 3 and 4, it is argued that if you want to know why it costs ninety cents today to ride in a New York subway car that was made in Japan, whereas it cost only a dime to ride in an American-made car in 1946, you are better off looking at changes in the international division of labor than at changes in the world money supply for an answer.

THE IMPERIAL DISCIPLINE

The maxim that the division of labor is limited by the extent of the market has been heralded as the most fruitful generalization in the history of economics. It may be so, even if it does read as well backward as forward. But this tenet is also why complexity is of very little interest to economists. If the division of labor is determined by markets, economists have reasoned, then never mind specialization itself. Instead, study markets. In markets, complexity counts for nothing; the interplay of supply and demand is all. A greater complexity of the division of labor means only that the market has broadened, a difference between one equilibrium point and another.

Now it is a fact of overwhelming significance that equilibrium analysis seems to work; that is, it has great power to explain and to predict what actually happens in markets. In some deep sense, markets are not *like* systems in equilibrium; they *are* systems in equilibrium. But it is also true that this vision of the economy as a general equilibrium system confers an extraordinary rhetorical advantage on economists. It permits them to bring the most sophisticated and austere forms of mathematical analysis to bear on their subject. Perhaps for this reason more than any other, economists generally have monopolized the discussion of the manner in which specialization proceeds, foreclosing others who may have something to say. Who else can describe the economy with so much rigor and precision? Who else can "explain" so wide a range of phenomena—nothing less than what is produced, how it is produced, and how it is distributed?

True, there has been an undercurrent of concern with the division of labor in the writings of Alexis de Tocqueville, Karl Marx, Max Weber, and Emile Durkheim. But all of them took Adam Smith as their point of departure, and none volunteered an apparatus for thinking about specialization that could take the place of the market hypothesis—though goodness knows, Karl Marx tried!

Tocqueville, for example, echoed concerns that had been broached by Smith: "As the principle of the division of labor is more extensively applied, the workman becomes more weak, more narrow-minded and more dependent. . . . The art advances, the artisan recedes."

Marx, who powerfully chronicles the increase in the division of labor in the sixteenth century, finds quite a different prospect. Though he seems to be acutely aware of another increase in his own time, he nevertheless seems to have thought the division of labor would go away after the next revolution. His writing on the topic is almost impossible to follow closely, but in his emphasis on classes and hierarchies, and in his distinctions between the technological division of task and the economic division of labor, he is always interesting.

Unlike Marx, Max Weber thought that specialization was here to stay, though he believed it had created an "iron cage" of increasing rationalization that imprisoned modern men. For him, the "means of production" were not so interesting as the "means of administration"; bureaucracy was as much an independent juggernaut as capitalism, "expert officialdom" as significant a specimen of the division of labor as the *rentier* and the merchant. The continuing imperative to specialize was all the more painful, Weber thought, since it had lost the spiritual underpinnings that had set it in motion. "The Puritan wanted to work in a calling; we are forced to do so," he writes at the end of *The Protestant Ethic and the Spirit of Capitalism*. "Of this last stage of cultural development, it might well be truly said, 'Specialists without vision, sensualists without heart; this nullity imagines that it has attained a level of civilization never before achieved.' "

And Durkheim, though he railed against the methodological failings of the "exchangists," meaning the economists, thought that specialization was a splendid process that was delivering men from the ignominy of village life. Taking the opposite tack from Tocqueville and Marx, he reasoned that men would lead fuller lives once they were freed from the "organic solidarity" of the primitive community. The division of labor permitted each person to become "a thorough and complete human being, one quite sufficient unto himself," rather than remaining the mere "organ of an organism."

Taken together, however, the strains of sociology and anthropology that grew from these writings have contributed very little to a better understanding of the processes of economic development. None of the writers mentioned above succeeded in making it a central concern to his followers. To give credit where it is due, the idea of complexity is implicit in Marx; he is the progenitor of the tradition in which economies are viewed as essentially cumulative, transitive, connective social formations, as a matter of fabric rather than of balance. (This emphatically is not to say that a call to revolution lurks at the end of this book. On the contrary, the view here is that the revolution has been going on all around us, all the time.) From the Marxists, however, there has been no real attempt to write the history of the division of labor. Instead, the impulse has come from historians of science, business, medicine, and other fields. Money and economic development are almost exclusively the province of economists, and economists are not interested in specialization. The result is that serious theorizing about complexity is only now coming in.

MEASURING SPECIALIZATION

The idea of economic complexity requires a fairly rigorous notion of the meaning of an economic niche or specialty, but so what? Such a concept should be fairly easy to develop. It is hard to decide where to draw the line between niches, especially when a new specialization is emerging, but there is always difficulty knowing where to draw lines. Looking backward, there is a clear enough distinction between a general manager and an executive committee member, between a controlman who tends a continuous steel caster and a pourer on an open hearth furnace, and between a microsurgeon and an orthopedist. The point is that the idea of economic complexity gives us a *fundamental* way of talking about the different-partedness of an economy.

To be sure, complexity will not submit to the "measuring rod of money." It requires a different kind of yardstick or metric, one known among experts as equivalency classes. Let me sketch a very simple example of the kind of metric that will suit its measurement. Hotels and restaurants are often rated according to their economic complexity, with one star for no frills, two stars for tourist class, three stars for business class, four stars for resort class, five stars for luxury class, and so on. These distinctions are based ultimately on the number of different kinds of services that are provided. In the no-frills hotel, you make your own bed; in the luxury hotel, a maid not only makes your bed in the morning but comes around to turn it down at night. In a luxury hotel, there are more different kinds of jobs than in the simple place. These are very simple equivalency classes, but they resemble the more sophisticated distinctions used to measure the complexity of much more complicated systems, such as computers. In time, these more sophisticated measures will be adapted for the discussion of the complexity of economic systems. In the meantime, we will get by with intuitively obvious equivalency classes like those now in use; we will talk about "developing nations" and "less developed countries," "industrial nations," "service economies," and "post-industrial society." The best currently available rough indicator of the complexity of the economy is a standard industrial classification (SIC) code, a kind of Yellow Pages for the nation. It is the SIC code that classifies the American economy into ten divisions (agriculture, mining, construction, manufacturing, transportation, wholesale trade, retail trade, finance, services, and public administration), then breaks it down into eight-hundred-odd major groups (mining and quarrying of nonmetallic minerals except fuels, for example, or fabricated structural metal products), and finally into nearly ten thousand industries (dimension stone, cordage and twine, and so on).

Thus we speak of one-digit, two-digit, three-digit, and four-digit SIC code classifications, the way we might speak of levels of resolution of a lens. When combined with a frequent census of industries, in which firms must fit themselves into the SIC code, the classification scheme becomes a powerful measurement device.

Naturally, SIC codes have problems of their own. As Anne Carter, an economist who is an expert on input-output analysis, has put it, "The object of any classification scheme is to group objects into categories. As new items are produced, the job of classification is to group the new with old ones. Are guided missiles 'ordnance' or 'aircraft'? Is the molding of fiberglass 'plastic products' or 'boatbuilding'? Whatever the new item, it is bound to start out as a small one and to be tucked into an old category—until it becomes large enough—old enough—to warrant category space of its own." Also, Carter notes, there is no way to differentiate quality in a classification scheme: cars, chemicals, and computers may be quite different today from what they were twenty years ago, but the industries that deliver them still have the same labels.

It is only when the SIC code is merged with an occupational dictionary that a truly three-dimensional picture of the extent of the division of labor—of the complexity of the economy—begins to emerge. "Specialties" or "jobs" or "niches" and not firms are the ultimate building blocks of the complexity of an economy. It should be clear that a pirate, a pickpocket's "drop," a cocaine dealer, or a counterfeiter is as much a specialist as is a podiatrist or a telephone lineman. Varying degrees of complexity are as much a feature of the underground economy as the legitimate one, and the two can be thought of only in connection with one another. Marx was right: the criminal *is* a producer of the system of criminal justice.

What light does the SIC code cast on the growing complexity of the economy over time? The simplest observation is that the service sector is growing. The composition of American employment in 1870, by highly aggregated sectors determined from the SIC code, was 47 percent agricultural, 27 percent industrial, and 27 percent in services; in 1970 it was 4 percent agricultural, 39 percent industrial, and 57 percent in services. What is striking in the census of industries over these hundred years is that instead of shrinking in absolute numbers, almost every sector of the economy has grown substantially in the numbers of jobs it contained; steel may no longer be the center of the economy, as it once was, but it remains an important industry. Surely this growth and diversification are the essence of what has happened to the world economy in the past eighty years. Yet economics textbooks, simple and advanced, do not mention the SIC code, nor do they concern themselves with the theory behind it. Perhaps not surprisingly, the classification system's best friends are marketing executives who rely on it to identify likely targets for sales. Economists simply take it for granted.

The display of SIC data is cumbersome. Can the complexity characteristics of an economy be described in any better way? In Chapter 5 we catch a glimpse of a community of researchers who think so. The parameters of complexity are like the parameters for human measurement. There are perhaps many, but not hundreds. There is every reason to think that economic complexity can be explicitly modeled in the same way, the essential characteristics caught, the detail omitted. If it is possible to describe computers concisely, it ought to be possible to describe an industry and its customers. In the meantime, though, a recent SIC code and an industry census will be metrically sufficient for considering economic complexity in most cases.

A HIERARCHY OF COMPLEXITY

Notice that complexity is not just a property of big economic systems. The word discloses a whole family of terms. In each case, the concept has to do with the number of different components and the number of interfaces between them, and in the end, economic complexity turns out to be fundamentally hierarchical. That is, a complex economy is comprised of various combinations of tasks, jobs, products, businesses, and industries, all of which may vary in their complexity, starting with the individual worker.

For example, a space suit is a more complex garment than a business suit, and an automobile is a more complex mode for travel than a bicycle. With suitable attempts to qualify exactly what kind of a product we are talking about, we may speak of product complexity. Computers, airplanes, bombs, and telephone service have all become more complex since the end of World War II.

Complex products require complex organizations to produce them: a symphony is more complex than a quintet, and it takes many more people to produce it. Because of this, there must be high volume to sustain a sophisticated product like an auto, or high prices to sustain a sophisticated product like an opera.

Even the most apparently simple product can in fact be quite complex. Theodore Levitt has shown that even so apparently simple a product as durum wheat has a rich array of characteristics of significance to its purchasers, including its protein, moisture, farina, and gluten content, to say nothing of delivery date and assurability of supply. "Products are almost always combinations of the tangible and the intangible," writes Levitt, who is a most imaginative analyst of complexity. "An automobile is not simply a machine for movement, visibly or measurably differentiated by design, size, color, options, horsepower or miles per gallon. It is also a complex symbol denoting status, taste, rank, achievement, aspiration and (these days) being 'smart'—that is, buying fuel economy rather than display." Levitt concludes that there is simply no such thing as a commodity. All goods and services are differentiable, he says, and the path to success often involves investing commodities with characteristics they formerly weren't known to have. (Economists often treat goods of different qualities simply as wholly different goods, which is another way of dismissing complexity. This can lead to problems. As Keith B. Leffler puts it, "When quality is variable and the costs of measuring complex products are not zero, casually applied supply-and-demand analysis will likely lead to incorrect predictions.")

To managers, there is the matter of the complexity of a particular business or industry. At the height of the Bendix–Martin Marietta takeover battle, for example, Thomas Taylor, an analyst at the Wall Street investment banking firm of Legg Mason Wood, said, "It's like having a company that makes filters take over the Chrysler Corporation. Just because you know how to make filters doesn't mean you know how to run a big complex systems company." He meant that the number of Martin Marietta's connections with suppliers, customers, competitors, product designers, and all the others were of a different order of magnitude than those of Bendix—a point it is hard to doubt.

Complexity crops up at the simplest levels of economic life, as task complexity and job complexity. Indeed, the design of work promises to be one of the most fruitful areas of inquiry into complexity. Some jobs are simple, others complex, and even the simplest seem to have much latitude in their design. Take the operation of a turret lathe, for example. Peter Albin has shown how the tasks involved can vary widely in autonomy and richness. His conclusion is that more complex is better, at least where job satisfaction is concerned. Optimal levels of complexity can lead to healthier, happier, and more productive workers.

WHY IT'S HARD TO SEE

There are certain reasons that changes in the degree of complexity are hard to gauge. Simple spatial considerations have something to do with it. You don't know what you can't see.

For example, when at the turn of the century Upton Sinclair wrote about hog slaughter in *The Jungle*, it seemed especially advanced. ("He had dressed hogs himself in the forests of Lithuania, but he had never expected to live to see one hog dressed by several hundred men.") Sinclair stressed the extent of the yards, their bleakness, the spectacle of square miles of yards without a single green plant. But the division of labor was still a local thing. Men tossed the offal in the lake and went home to their South Side cottages in the evening.

Today, the specialization in hog farming starts much earlier and ends much later. The modern pig climbs on the assembly line at birth, lives its entire life indoors, is fed a computer-formulated diet loaded with vitamin and mineral supplements, and goes to the slaughterhouse five months later. Instead of having his throat cut by a man, he is stunned with a hammer and killed by a jolt of electricity, often as not generated by a nuclear power plant.

This is not simply more complex technology; the inventions involved also require a more complex division of labor to make them work. The inspector who checks the meat, like the inspector who checks the lake, relies on sophisticated instrumentation, and these machines, like the killing apparatus, are built by workers far from the slaughterhouses.

To be sure, the hog butcher to the world is no longer Chicago. The feedlots on the south side of the city have been leveled; in their place are empty lots, decaying public housing, and a high-tech research center. If you were to judge by the absence of bustle there, you would say the world had grown less complex, not more. In fact, the slaughterhouses are still miracles of efficiency, but they have pulled back even farther from major urban centers, leaving Chicago for Amarillo and Sioux City —just as a hundred years before they left Cambridge's Porter Square and New York's Gansevoort Street for Chicago. Elsewhere, out of sight, the complexity has grown, and Swift and Armour, once the epitome of organizational complexity, have become small cogs in large industrial machines.

Notice, too, that from wherever you sit inside an organization, its complexity seems to be about the same. Herbert Simon has noted that "the complexity of an army, as viewed by its commanding general, or of the United States Steel Corporation, as viewed by its president, is no greater than the complexity of a regiment or a rolling mill, when these are viewed from the positions of those who manage them. A manager, no matter how large or small his total responsibility, interacts closely with a few subordinates, a few superiors, and a few coordinate managers. The number of people with whom he communicates is approximately the same, whatever his level in the total organization."

WHAT COMPLEXITY ISN'T

In thinking about complexity, it is important not to confuse the complexity of an economy with the experience of living in it. Living in the world often gets simpler as the world gets more complex. To hear one of Bach's Brandenburg Concertos, for example, it is no longer necessary to hire a hall and an orchestra or to wait for a concert to be given. All you need to do is put a record on the phonograph.

But in terms of the specialization required to bring about the event, the modern situation of music is far more complex than it was Bach's time. Then, the music industry consisted mainly of instrument makers, musicians, kings, and choirmasters. Today it includes lawyers, finance capitalists, executive producers, distributors, salesmen, advertising specialists, and retailers, to say nothing of the manufacturers of polyvinyl chloride, turntables, and electricity. And of course it is still necessary to assemble the orchestra and perhaps a musical historian knowledgeable in the conventions of Bach's time. Moreover, every year or so, some new would-be specialist comes along with a new invention (a synthesizer, digital recorder, lightweight personal tape player, and a new musical style are a few) to make the musical scene more complex still.

It is also important not to confuse the idea of economic complexity with problems that may or may not be associated with it. It is true, as Thomas Haskell has argued, that a sense of causation recedes as interdependence grows. People feel less in control of their lives when the division of labor is great. It is true, too, that as complexity grows, there seems to be a "thinner life of things," in Daniel Boorstin's evocative phrase for the attenuation of meaning that has accompanied modern life. (I like to think of the difference between the simple old major leagues of baseball, two leagues of eight teams each concentrated in ten eastern and midwestern cities—and the complex modern major leagues, twenty-six teams in four divisions spread throughout the North American continent.) Once, when I was expounding complexity at a seminar in New York, a young economist chimed in, "You are not talking about complexity, you mean alienation!"

He was wrong, dead wrong. Whether or not alienation increases as the division of labor becomes more complex is a fascinating issue, but it is not my topic. I'm interested in the increasing division of labor and its price level consequences—and in why the topic hasn't been explored before.

3

COST WEBS AND EVERYDAY PRICES

DURING THE 1950S AND 1960S, ECONOMISTS, BUSINESSMEN, and even bureaucrats noticed something curious: health care costs were rising much faster than the consumer price index. The price of a day in a hospital climbed from $16 in 1950 to $214 by 1978, an increase of some 1,200 percent—in a period when the price of a Popsicle increased only from 5 to 30 cents and the consumer price index itself increased only 171 percent. What was the reason for this spectacular rise? There were a number of theories. Some analysts insisted that there were too few hospitals, shortage being the usual explanation for rising prices; after all, if banana prices were going up much faster than the CPI, the story would be that there were bottlenecks in their production amid rising demand. Others said that modern medicine was simply technologically backward and wasn't getting the same productivity gains as the rest of the economy, banana picking included. Another group argued that hospital managers had let wage bills get out of hand. This was a "cost push" explanation, the same that would be applied to banana prices if there were a banana pickers' union. But 1,200 percent? Where were the nurses' yachts?

Then, starting in the early 1970s, a young scholar named Martin Feldstein transformed our understanding of the problem. As a graduate student, Feldstein had wanted to be a doctor. After a year at Oxford, he became an economist instead. He investigated the problem of soaring medical bills and was surprised by what he found.

Feldstein learned that it wasn't short supply, sloppy usage, or overgenerous wage bargaining that was causing the health care price spiral. Instead, he discovered that the hospital bed was no longer just a cranked-up cot in a clean white room. It came attached—through its daily price tag—to intensive care wards, CAT scanners, kidney dialysis machines, malpractice awards, and batteries of defensive diagnostic tests designed to forestall malpractice suits. Hospital managers marked up the per diem price of a bed to cover all the gear and services they were buying, insurance companies rubber-stamped the bills, and people went on taking health insurance from their employers instead of wage boosts because they didn't have to pay taxes on insurance benefits. Although this extraordinary burst of technical change and its effect on prices had been entirely overlooked by other analysts, Feldstein felt it was the answer to the exploding price problem. "Cost inflation in hospital care does not mean that consumers are paying much more for the same old product," he writes. "It means they are buying a different and much more expensive product. Hospital cost inflation is therefore quite different from other types of inflation." Using sophisticated econometric modeling techniques, he proved this to the satisfaction of his fellow economists.

The kind of "complexity inflation" Feldstein found in health care has not attracted widespread attention among economists. It isn't mentioned in the textbooks along with those better-known "types" of inflation, "cost-push" and "demand-pull." Yet perhaps it is a far more common variety of "inflation" than is often supposed. In this chapter, in situations large and small, we shall find precisely the kind of relationship among complexity, prices, and money that Feldstein identified in health care.

We will introduce a useful conceptual tool—the cost web—as a resort whenever we are confronted with quickly rising everyday prices. Indeed, it may be that in learning to think about the role of increasing complexity in the problem of rising prices, we will significantly alter our understanding of the problem, for hospital cost inflation really isn't inflation at all.

THE THEORY DECIDES . . .

Looking back, especially from a viewpoint outside the discipline of economics, it seems quite plain that the rise of new methods and machines had much to do with driving up the price of hospital care. We smile when we think of the scholars who earnestly argued that a shortage of hospitals or technical backwardness was at the root of the price spiral. Yet the shelves of libraries are lined with crumbling books and pamphlets that argue just that.

This episode is eloquent testimony to the ability of the ideas we learn from textbooks to govern our perception of events. Einstein said that theory decides what we can observe. He meant that what we expect to see governs where we look; that what we see must correspond to "filing bins" for various experiences that have already been established in our minds. If what we see fits these preconceived categories, it is filed away. If it doesn't fit, we more often than not simply fail to see it. Breaking away from the theory is never easy; indeed, simply "breaking away" cannot be done. Only a new theory, a better filing system, can replace one that is already in use. You can't escape *from* a theory; you can only go on to a better one.

In economics, there are theories—two conceptual filing bins —for dealing with rising prices. One is the familiar apparatus of supply and demand, in which rising prices signal the need for more production and lead to a decline in consumption. This is the essence of Equilibrium Theory. The other tool is the conceptual apparatus of inflation and deflation. In this scheme of things—the Quantity Theory of Money that was discussed earlier—rising prices are a sign that the money supply is growing faster than the supply of goods and services.

At first, Feldstein tries to fit the case of health care into the standard vocabulary of equilibrium analysis, but describing what had happened in terms of supply and demand came perilously close to doubletalk. It was true, Feldstein writes, that the economic analysis of ordinary markets emphasizes that prices rise because supply does not increase as rapidly as demand. "But in the case of hospitals," he explains, "I think the opposite is true. It is precisely because supply has kept pace with demand that hospital costs have gone up." This approach is not very promising to those who are fond of the English language. What it means is that you could rule out the "bottleneck" explanation; high prices didn't mean that there were too many sick people and too few places to treat them.

So instead, Feldstein zeros in on what is essentially a monetarist explanation for the health care cost spiral—but with a significant modification. It was the widespread availability of insurance money to pay hospital bills that was the real reason for the spiral, he says; what was unusual was that instead of too much money chasing too few goods, it was too much money causing too much complexity in the form of ever more sophisticated care. Usually, he says, inflation means paying more and more for the same old thing. In this case, it means paying for a more sophisticated basket: "Technological progress in hospitals does not involve making the old product more cheaply but making a new range of products that are more expensive."

The role of increasing complexity in causing higher prices didn't interest Feldstein nearly so much as the role of increasing money in causing complexity, however. "I believe that it is the method of financing health care services that primarily determines the pattern of technical change," he writes. "Hospitals would not be buying the latest, expensive medical technology if they could not afford it. What permits them to afford it is the mode of insuring against hospital costs." The solution to rising health care costs was to cut back on insurance. (It isn't possible to do justice here to the Swiss-watch precision of Feldstein's arguments.)

It was true, he notes, that this explanation raised an "awkward question." If it was merely a changing product that was driving health care prices up, rather than some kind of inefficiency, could the rising prices really be considered a "problem" at all? How much technical change or economic complexity is too much? The broad answer, Feldstein argues, was that the prepayment of insurance premiums distorted consumers' choices. The availability of all that insurance money encouraged hospitals to provide a more expensive product than consumers would wish to pay for (compared to all the other things they might want to buy instead if they were fully informed)— even though, in the end, "consumers do pay for it, in ever-higher insurance premiums," said Feldstein.

On one point Feldstein is adamant. It was the insurance money that elicited the complexity, not the other way around. "There are two—and really only two—key ingredients to understanding the rise in hospital costs: the changing nature of the hospital product, and the impact of insurance. Of these, the second is the more crucial, and largely explains the first," he writes. Louise Russell, another economic researcher, puts it even more firmly in a report for the Brookings Institution. She says, "But new technologies are only some of the things we spend money on, not the reason we spend it—a symptom, not a cause. The real reason for the rising costs is much more general and has to do with the growth of private health insurance and public programs like Medicare and Medicaid, referred to collectively as third-party payers."

Wait a minute. Would anyone but an economist think so?

WHY DO WE SPEND MONEY?

I talked to some doctors about the growth of the medical establishment in the past fifty years. Was it true, I asked, that the new technologies were only a means to the end of making money? Was it fair to say that dialysis, for example, was a "symptom" of the availability of insurance?

No, they said. On the contrary, it was the march of technical progress that was causing the insurance explosion. They ordered dialysis because it saved lives, they said, but as treatments became more advanced, more complex, and more effective, they became more expensive. Kidney dialysis costs at least $7,000 a year at home, twice or three times as much if it is done at the hospital. The cost of an open-heart procedure is around $15,000. A day in an intensive care unit costs several times as much as a day in an ordinary hospital bed, precisely because the ICU requires a far wider array of professional services, instrument makers, and attendants.

I observed that behind that new range of products and techniques stood a far more complex division of labor in health care than had existed in 1950. There were abundant numbers of new medical specialists, new clinical instrument makers, new salesmen, new "drug chemists," and new federal regulators. One could call them middlemen, specialists, intermediators, or whatever, yet wasn't it true that the price level in health care was a function of the number of different parts or niches in the system? The doctors were enthusiastic.

Yet, surely, medical complexity and insurance money are extremely interdependent. Nobody is completely free of the wish to earn his living. Take the case of malpractice insurance. Soaring malpractice awards were certainly part of the reason hospital prices were going up so fast. But where could we tear that web? Was it that doctors were fouling up more? Was it that lawyers had learned that insurance companies had deep pockets? Or was it simply that juries had become suddenly more sympathetic? Were big awards a result of the existence of big insurance bills? Or a cause? Could we answer this with any certainty?

For a masterful account of the rise of the American medical profession, with its attendant costs and benefits, that is quite at odds with the explanation derived from econometrics, it is helpful to read *The Social Transformation of American Medicine* by Paul Starr, a sociologist. It chronicles the creation of the market for health care—the division of labor that began in the nineteenth century when physicians began to replace the system of domestic care—and the subsequent unceasing efforts of physicians to consolidate their professional authority in order to win some independence from the market, with eventual success.

Can we say with real conviction whether *any* of the events in health care in the past fifty years were generated predominantly by the sellers of health care services or by the consumers? Can we really say that the pattern of financing determined the pattern of technical change? True, the sellers of health care had consistently come up with goods and services to offer the buying public, but hadn't those buyers also played a big role in demanding better treatment? Isn't it at least partly true that the demand for health care creates a supply of scientists, that doctors set out to conquer polio because they knew the public would pay for it? The health insurance industry clearly played a big part in facilitating the growth of the health care sector until its magnitude in the American economy was surpassed only by that of the defense sector. But did it *cause* this growth? Let us call this the "direction of causation" problem. We shall see more of it as we go along.

GOLD-PLATING

From a purely descriptive viewpoint, it doesn't matter whether greater complexity arises from the demand side (buyers who want to be cured) or supply side (sellers who want to do a land office business) or from an increase in the quantity of money. It is the underlying fact of greater complexity that counts. If you're not paying more for the same old thing, you don't want to call this particular phenomenon of rising prices "inflation." Call it complexification, hypertrophy, intermediation, bundling, or something else. But be careful what you call it, because *it* takes place in other fields, too. One of the best-known examples is defense procurement.

In *National Defense*, James Fallows tells—as an analogy representing modern weaponry—the story of a certain flashlight developed by the Air Force during the 1960s. At first it was a simple flashlight for pilots to carry. Then it became a flashing flashlight, so that downed pilots could signal in code. Then a red light was added to protect pilots' night vision. Naturally, it was also specified that it work at the North Pole and in the Sahara—requirements that added to its bulk. By the time it had been developed, the Air Force flashlight cost far more than commercial ones, was too heavy to fit in a flight suit, and was largely inoperable.

In its most obvious form, this tendency toward complexity is called "gold-plating," but the complexity that has been driving the defense cost spiral is far more than skin deep. Not only has the kind of army we field become far more complex, but so have the weapons with which it is equipped. As a result, the prices of such things as tanks and ships have soared much faster than the consumer price index. In real terms, the Army was spending as much on tanks in 1983 as it had during the Korean War, but the same sum of money when adjusted for inflation bought only 701 tanks in 1983 against 6,735 tanks in 1953. The same could be said about ships, planes, and even rifles. The price of a Navy destroyer has, like the cost of a day in the hospital, escalated far faster than the CPI, and for the same reasons—the new machines are far more complex than the old, and they were manufactured in an economy that was generally more complex.

Notice that the same terms of the debate over health care apply to defense spending: It may be, to paraphrase the reasoning Louise Russell applied to health care, that the "new weapons are just some of the things we spend money on, not the reason we spend it—the symptom, not the cause." But it trivializes the arms race to say that it exists merely because the Defense Department is willing to pay for it. The growth of military complexity is a far subtler process than that of money burning a hole in Pentagon pockets.

WHO PAYS THE BILLS?

What, then, does drive the military price spiral? James Fallows locates the tendency toward gold-plating and hypercomplexity in poor management and bad strategy. Mary Kaldor, in her fine book *The Baroque Arsenal,* accuses the arms merchants of contriving the race. Anthony Sampson, the sophisticated author of *The Arms Bazaar,* contributes the memorable formulation that the arms race isn't between the Americans and the Russians but rather between Boeing and Lockheed. I think each of them is partly right.

I think it is also partly true that the simple technological possibilities themselves sometimes govern the process, as in medicine. It was Einstein, after all, who urged Roosevelt to build the atomic bomb, not the Du Pont Company, which actually built it. Similar temptations have arisen as military planners have realized the extraordinary military possibilities of the chip. The overriding fact about the arms race is that it is a *race.* There are two parties involved, and at any particular moment either one can make a powerful case to itself that the other is somehow ahead. How much of the current arms race is technologically driven is anybody's guess, but certainly much of it is. The military implications of the rocket, the laser, and the semiconductor chip are as striking as those of the atomic bomb, and, in the atmosphere of mutual distrust, to conceive of a weapon is almost always to be required to build it.

It is also partly true, I think, that there is something to be said for the sort of "monetary" interpretation of "defense cost inflation" that was devised for health care—but not very much. It is true that arms theorists know that Congress has deep pockets, but to argue that the W-2 form caused the arms race is more than a little one-sided.

Certainly it is legitimate to ask how much of the tendency toward gold-plating and hypercomplexity arises because of the kind of marketplace that exists for atom bombs and CAT scanners. There is plenty of resemblance between the two. Like medical technology, weapons are dauntingly complicated, which means that the persons for whom they are ordered—the citizens, like the patients in the health care situation—don't understand them. (Economists call this a problem in "asymmetrical information.") It means, too, that there is a temptation on the part of those who do understand these systems—the people who design and buy them—to want to create the most ambitious designs possible, replete with "bells and whistles," as the saying goes. Finally, when contractors work on a cost-plus basis, they have little incentive to hold down wages or overhead and their customers have little incentive to watch them. After all, it is not the designers' and purchasers' money that is being spent; it is the insurance companies' and the Congress's. This feature of their markets—what economists call "third-party payment" and the rest of us call "deep pockets"—is perhaps the most important aspect that health care and defense procurement have in common.

But at bottom, who can doubt that it is greater complexity—a fundamental "change in the product"—and not waste or cupidity that is the key to understanding higher prices? The lack of competition between providers is not the reason a CAT scanner or a nuclear submarine is expensive. All the price cutting in the world will not bring the cost of a B-1 bomber in line with that of a Piper Cub. Nor does bureaucratic bungling explain very much.

Moreover, third-party payment systems may be prone to mediocrity, but they are not necessarily condemned to it. Take Hyman Rickover and his nuclear submarines or Robert Moses and his Triborough Bridge. Using tolls collected from the bridge, Moses proceeded to build other toll bridges and tunnels. He created a torrent of cash, with which he then built parks, aqueducts, beaches, and tunnels—in effect "gold-plating" New York. The fact that these programs were smoothly run didn't keep them from being expensive.

The interesting thing is that the same Martin Feldstein who criticized the health care establishment so knowledgeably was, as chairman of the Council of Economic Advisors, one of the foremost defenders of the Reagan administration's military budget. Presumably he immersed himself in its details; presumably he knew that defense prices are rising even more sharply than health care costs—and that a "change in the product" is a large part of the reason.

Feldstein has yet to transfer his insights from health care to defense, however. He has yet to say that technological process in weaponry does not mean making the old product more cheaply but making a new range of products that are more expensive. He has yet to observe that military cost inflation, like hospital cost inflation, is quite different from other types of rising prices. And, most significant, he has yet to say that it is the endless appropriations of Congress that "cause" the military cost explosion—and that therefore the way to control the defense price spiral is to limit appropriations.* We wouldn't be buying atom bombs if we couldn't afford them, either, but we choose to pay the price because we believe that we would be at an intolerable strategic disadvantage without nuclear weapons. Mightn't the same thing be said about CAT scanners?

COST WEBS

Clearly there is a problem in thinking about these intricate relationships between patterns of manufacture and patterns of finance when "supply of" and "demand for" are your only ana-

---

* This can be taken to extremes: Did the invention of the income tax cause the growth of government? There are people who believe this, one of the earliest having been Edmund Wilson, who presented the proposition in his pioneering essay "The Cold War and the Income Tax." These are generally the same people who believe that the best way to cut spending is to cut taxes. Martin Feldstein is their cheerleader.

lytic tools. In order to describe long chains of economic connection such as those in health care and defense, and to keep firmly in mind their disparate parts, I propose that we take a leaf from the ecologists' books and describe them schematically. When ecologists encounter a complex community of living things, they sometimes simplify the intricate relationships between species of plants and animals by describing who eats whom. They call the resulting diagram a food web, and any linear sequence in it is a food chain.

Somewhat analogously, Figure 1 describes the rough outline of the health care business as Feldstein found it. The important players and their relationships are described in terms of who buys from whom. At the bottom left are consumers, who pay for their care through premiums paid to insurance funds, private firms, semiprivate agencies (like Blue Cross), and public plans (like Medicare and Medicaid). Employers' contributions are also paid into the funds, often in lieu of wages. The insur-

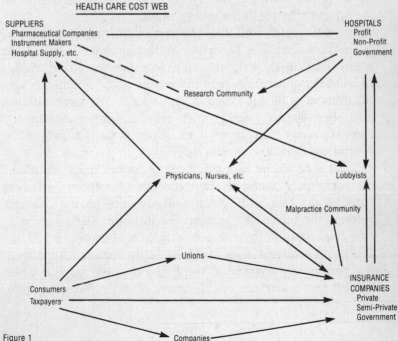

HEALTH CARE COST WEB

Figure 1

ance companies in turn pay hospitals of various sorts. The physicians' support comes from all three sources: they are employed individually by patients and by hospitals, and they do a certain amount of work that is directly compensated by insurance companies. Some unions negotiate for paraprofessionals and blue-collar workers who are involved in the provision of health care; other unions bargain for health care benefits for consumers of medical benefits. In the upper-left-hand corner are the businesses that, according to Feldstein's account, have been the prime beneficiaries of the insurance companies, at least for the past thirty years: the pharmaceutical companies, the instrument makers, the pacemaker companies, the dialysis firms, and others. Important, but somewhat more tenuously linked to the beneficiaries' group, is the research community. And of course there are the omnipresent lobbyists: for the American Medical Association, the American Hospital Association, the insurance companies, the pharmaceutical houses, and so on. All are shown in the figure, linked by arrows that show the direction in which the money flows.

I suggest that we call this type of schematic representation of the relationships in a particular industrial community a "cost web." Particularly helpful would be estimates of the magnitudes of the dollar flows between sectors of the community and the number of jobs involved in each sector. We may let dotted lines show channels along which influence rather than money flows. In many cases, it would be helpful actually to list the ten biggest organizations in each category.

What is gained by such a depiction? For one thing, a sense of the complexity of the relevant economic "universe." Also, a sense of the ease with which a disturbance in one area can redound throughout the system. For instance, dialysis technology, originating in the research sector, could grow to a $10-billion-a-year industry in just ten years only because so relatively few persons are involved in the decision to purchase it. They suggest how crucial the establishment of some third-party payment system can be for the practitioners of a primary business, such as dentists or veterinarians.

The most important thing about cost webs, however, is that they give a strong impression of just how many different influences are exerted on everyday prices. They add a third implement to the two primary tools of economic analysis; they open a window on economic complexity. Without immediately thinking about supply and demand, without worrying about the behavior of the central bank and our monetary theory, we may ask what is really happening to make everyday prices soar. And more often than not, we will discover it is something that has to do with the economic complexity of the system.

Another thing to be said for cost webs is that they present a clear sense of how intimately public and private enterprises are connected. Figure 2 is another cost web, in effect a cross section of the military-industrial complex at a very high level of

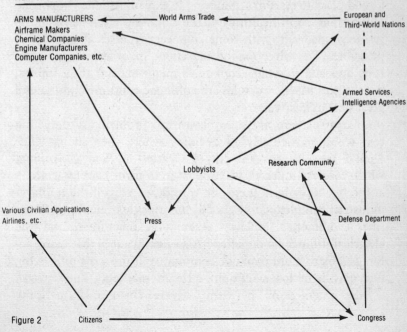

WEAPONS INDUSTRY COST WEB

ARMS MANUFACTURERS ◄——— World Arms Trade ◄——— European and Third-World Nations
Airframe Makers
Chemical Companies
Engine Manufacturers
Computer Companies, etc.

Armed Services, Intelligence Agencies

Lobbyists

Research Community

Various Civilian Applications. Airlines, etc.

Press

Defense Department

Figure 2   Citizens ———————————————► Congress

aggregation. It depicts the relationships between the U.S. Congress, the Defense Department, the armed forces, foreign governments, arms merchants, weapons theorists, and other related groups. In the lower-left-hand corner is the taxpayer, whose taxes rise and fall with congressional appropriations. He is, presumably, the ultimate beneficiary of the system. In the lower-right-hand corner is Congress, the administrator, whose support in turn goes to the Defense Department and the armed forces, the third-party payers in the system. Because the procurement of weapons has much to do with global strategy—with whether a particular fighter aircraft can be sold to Turkey or Brazil or not—the policies of other nations enter into the process intimately. Finally, in the upper-left-hand corner is the industrial complex itself: the airframe makers and chemical companies, engine manufacturers and computer firms, an astonishingly diverse and complex universe of corporations. The literature on the mainspring of the military-industrial complex is extensive, and there is little agreement; still, a cost web seems a good place to start in attempting to explain its inner workings. Notice that, as in health care, the rumbling often starts in the research quadrant, with some engineers' guesses about what is plausible. The direction of causation, in other words, often runs opposite to what economists might expect: the supplier, not the purchaser (much less the ultimate consumer), initiates a great deal of change.

Of course there are many empirical problems in depicting cost webs, particularly in deciding where they should end. Should the city government of Charleston, South Carolina, which receives much of its support from taxes paid by workers at the big Navy base there, be considered part of the military-industrial complex? How should the triangle of nuclear submarines, commercial nuclear reactor manufacturers, and the electrical utilities be depicted? Also significant is that many actors belong to more than one community at the same time (a big firm may be in dozens of quite different markets). The strength of the interactions between players changes dramatically through time, in keeping with the business cycle and other rhythms. Nor are all interactions equally strong. And so on. Cost webs are, in effect, maps, and they carry their drawbacks and failings.

Yet my hunch is that cost webs will turn out to be more than merely descriptive. The ecologist Stuart Pimm argues that food webs are not the "tangled knitting" or "spaghetti" they appear to be. Their structures are "shaped by a limited number of biological processes," he says. In the same way, cost webs will turn out to display certain regularities—relationships between the vigor of third-party payment systems and the complexity of primary providers, for example—that are not necessarily the ones current theory leads us to expect.

Like SIC codes, cost webs cannot be found in economics textbooks or journals; they have no place in a science concerned almost exclusively with discovering the equilibrium that theory dictates as being the important aspect of economic situations. (The flow-of-funds analyses that are published by the Federal Reserve System, like much else that stems from input-output analysis, comes close to being a cost-web approach without ever quite breaking its ties to the concept of general equilibrium.) As guides to real communities of firms and to the ways in which they interact, however, cost webs may prove to be highly valuable, and I hope they find a place in economic analysis.

LONG-DISTANCE GOLD-PLATING

The relationship among economic complexity, everyday prices, and money obviously applies in the case of hospital costs and defense spending, in which a burgeoning complexity is clearly visible in the product. But there are products whose nature doesn't seem to change at all, yet they are important components of processes that could be described as "gold-plating schemes." Take oil, for example, a product that doesn't change a bit from year to year. A 1983 gallon of gas at $1.25 is, after all, no different from a 1963 gallon at 35 cents. A clearer example of paying "a lot more money for the same old thing" is hard to imagine. Or is it?

When gas was selling for 35 cents, everybody understood that 10 cents of the price of every gallon went, right off the top, to the federal government for highway construction. In a similar way, a few pennies of the price of every gallon went to the governments of oil-producing countries for similar schemes —until 1973, that is. When the OPEC nations twice raised the price of oil during the 1970s, that once-modest share—the "off-take," it was called by the experts—soared to 25 cents or even 50 cents a gallon. The crucial thing to understand here is that the money spent on gas wasn't simply "a lot more money for the same old thing." Instead, it was being used for projects that increased complexity throughout the oil-producing world—the construction of everything from AWAC planes to gambling casinos through new oil-prospecting equipment.

Is it too much to conceive of OPEC as a third-party payment system, analogous to health insurance or taxation for defense? Surely not. One theory has it that OPEC was in fact a scheme devised in a Georgetown basement in the 1950s for putting a military bulwark along the southern rim of Russia in order to replace the retreating British with sturdy Iranians and doughty Saudis. Others believe that it was the arms companies who gave vital aid and advice to OPEC in the course of seeking new markets; they were certainly among the biggest beneficiaries. What was the role of the oil companies? Or the banks? Is there a better way to regard OPEC than as a kind of forced Marshall Plan, in which the industrial nations financed the development—the complexification—of fifteen emergent industrial nations?

As in the case of hospitals and defense, we are dealing with a very complicated community when we talk about the world energy trade. In Figure 3 I have sketched a cost web to describe this sector. There are the usual features. Consumers pass along money to utilities and oil companies, which in turn support a diverse universe of foreign governments and firms in which banks, Third World borrowers, arms suppliers, and capital construction companies are prominent stars in the firmament. The loop concerned with automobiles is not an insignificant part of the web: recall that the American highway system is financed substantially by a tax on the sale of gasoline. A particularly interesting triangle is formed by the dotted lines of influence that connect the arms merchants, the OPEC nations, and the U.S. government. A great amount of money and influence passes along these lines.

But never mind who called OPEC into creation and caused the great price shocks of the 1970s, at least for the purpose of this book. What is clear is that developments in one part of the web can influence prices in all the others. For a decade, while the high price of oil held, the oil-buying consumer was not paying for "the same old thing" when he went to the pump. Something new had been added: in this case, a lot of disparate sorts

ENERGY INDUSTRY COST WEB

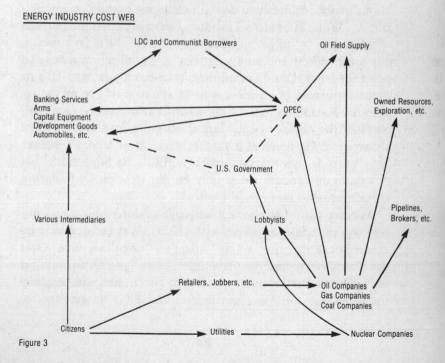

Figure 3

of "development." He was buying F-16s for the Iranians, London real estate for the Saudis, public education for the Kuwaitis, and a lot of modern exploration for the oil companies. "When I was 12, I studied by kerosene lamp. I drank water with little things moving in it from a clay jug. There was no doctor nearby," Mohammed H. Fayez, a construction manager for a Saudi construction company, told a reporter for *The New York Times*. "Today, my son thinks deprivation is a house in Jidda without a video."

But "gold-plated oil"? The sheer difficulty of talking about the relationship of complexity, prices, and money in the petroleum market suggests how hard it will be to establish an analytic framework in which these concepts fall into place. To a great extent, this is because of our dependence on the language of classical economics. "Monopoly profits" and "scarcity rents" are the main conceptual apparatus we've got when talking about OPEC, and neither conveys a very clear sense of the situation, which really has to do with changing patterns of specialization. When Harvard's Theodore Levitt says that the purpose of a business is "to get and keep customers," he is far closer to our sense of how and why a pattern of specialization arises and proceeds from the sale of oil than is an economist who tells us that the purpose of business is to "make money"; recall the remark by Karl Marx that the slave owner who increases his profits faces the choice of spending them on more slaves or more champagne: he finances a further division of labor, whatever his choice. It was the same with OPEC—the huge sums that flowed to oil vendors could only be put to work by financing specialization at home or abroad.

Another failure of classical language in describing a real system was especially apparent with OPEC. Was the dramatic increase in energy prices a "tax" hike or a "price" increase? Over the years, many analysts have referred to "the OPEC tax," if only because the revenues accrued to governments in precisely the same way the American federal excise tax on gasoline accrues to the highway trust. Indeed, the sudden shift in relative prices in 1973 "sucked a lot of purchasing power" out of the world economy, just as a U.S. tax increase might have. But those who registered it mainly as a price increase—and they included most of the advisers to the Ford administration in 1974—lobbied Congress that autumn for an income tax surcharge. The idea was to "fight inflation" by "sopping up excess purchasing power," and it was a little like throwing gasoline on a fire to put it out. In any event, when you buy a gallon of gas, you are contributing to the support of a new and far more variegated world economy, whether you want to or not, rather than paying "a lot more money for the same old thing."

This idea of "long-distance gold-plating" can illuminate any number of similar mechanisms in recent experience: the role of lawyers in the medical malpractice explosion, for example, or of clean-air legislation in the rising cost of electricity; of shoplifting as a factor in high supermarket prices or of graft in the cost of construction in New York. An investigation several years ago found that building costs were significantly higher in New York City because of payments to gangsters who had infiltrated the building trades. No one intends to pay the crooks' salaries, but through somewhat higher rents, construction costs, and other fees, we do.

MARKET-GENERATED COMPLEXITY

Nor is it simply brute power that enables middlemen to horn in at various points along the long and intricate chains of cost. Modern marketing has much to do with increasing the degree of complexity in order to broaden the market and with broadening the market through advertising and marketing in order to sustain complexity.

For a truly perceptive account of how complexity came to the National Basketball Association, for instance, read David Halberstam's *The Breaks of the Game*. He describes how the television networks—yet another third-party payer—drove up the price of tickets and cut the quality of the game in its search for a new way to sell cars, shaving cream, and beer. There were a number of reasons that people figured basketball would be "the game of the 1970s," but by the end of a decade of expansion, rather than being the same old sport, basketball had become something different, an "entertainment" industry rather than a game, complete with instant replays, rich ballplayers, and endless playoffs. The relevant cost web is in Figure 4. Here again, note the connection between public and private enterprise. What good is it to have an NBA franchise in town if the arena is too small to yield a profit?

As Halberstam observes, "What was happening to basketball was similar to what was happening to a great many products in America." There were wider markets, thanks to advances in transportation and communications; family firms in every con-

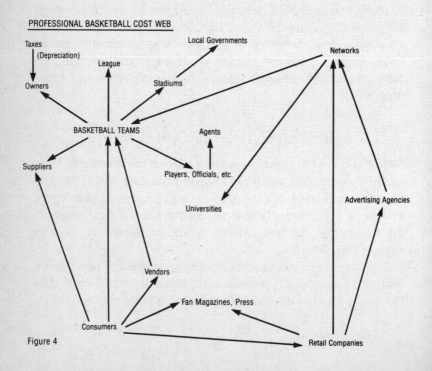

PROFESSIONAL BASKETBALL COST WEB

Figure 4

ccivable business, from newspapers to potato chips to high fashion, "went public" because of changing tax rules; relative prices shifted due to changing technologies (such as telephone costs coming down while mail prices went up); trade barriers were relaxed and foreign goods flooded the market. All these factors contributed to the burst of specialization that took place after World War II.

It is especially important to understand the role of consumer credit in facilitating the expansion of certain markets. Here again, a third-party payer—in this case the finance companies and banks—played a significant role, little different from the one played by the insurance companies with respect to health care, except that the banks spread out over time what the insurance companies spread out over the pool of those insured. The reader who is interested in these topics should search out Theodore Levitt's essays on corporate marketing practices, which offer the kind of "thick description" that the anthropologist Clifford Geertz made famous in describing more picturesque pursuits, such as the Balinese cockfight. In Levitt's view, product differentiation is the key to successful marketing, since it represents a response to potential customers that "give[s] them compelling reasons to want to do business with the originating supplier."

"To differentiate an offering effectively requires knowledge of what drives and attracts customers," writes Levitt. It "requires knowing how customers differ from one another and how those differences can be clustered into commercially meaningful segments. If you're not thinking segments, you're not thinking."

Is there a simple economic treatment of these considerations that will sweep away, like some bad dream, the problems that arise from complexity? I doubt it. Economic theory and language are strikingly impoverished on the subject of variations in the quality of goods. When thinking about the forces of supply and demand, economists usually prefer to think of the world as having been made new every moment. Attempts to grapple with the problem of variety, notably by Kelvin Lancaster, Columbia University's pioneering microeconomist, follow the insight of the famous dictum of Charles Revson, the lipstick magnate, who says: "In the factory, we manufacture cosmetics; in the store, we sell hope." In effect, economic analysis tries to understand the situation by studying the distribution of hope; here we try to understand it by dwelling on the history of the division of labor, in cosmetics manufacturing and every other human enterprise. The approaches are not contradictory; they complement one another.

THE DIRECTION OF CAUSATION REDUX

Always in addressing the question "Why did prices go up?" we have the problem of the "direction of causation." Prices went up in basketball because of increased complexity in the industry behind the game, but did complexity in basketball grow because there was money to be made? Or was there money to be made because people had discerned new ways of differentiating their products? An especially clear example of this chicken-and-egg type of problem can be found in the automobile business in its early years. Henry Ford used to tell customers, "You can have any color you want as long as it's black." For years, he also declined to arrange financing. He might have argued that the General Motors Acceptance Corporation caused the brand proliferation with which GM became synonymous and set off the spiral of rising auto prices by offering installment credit. ("Consumers wouldn't be buying the latest in automatic starters if they couldn't afford them. . . ." is the way Martin Feldstein might put it.)

Indeed, so deeply rooted in the human condition is this difference of opinion about the relationship of money and complexity that you can find Ralph Waldo Emerson and Henry Thoreau, those two irreconcilable poles of the spirit, arguing about it in the wake of the California gold rush. In 1854 Emerson recorded in his journal this exchange:

> Thoreau thinks 'tis immoral to dig gold in California; immoral to leave creating value, & go to augmenting the representative of value, & so altering and diminishing real value, &, that, of course, the fraud will appear.
>
> I consider that work to be as innocent as any other speculating. Every man should do what he can; & he was created to augment some real value, & not for a speculator. When he leaves or postpones (as most men do) his proper work & adopts some short or cunning method, as of watching markets, or farming in any manner the ignorance of the people, as, in buying by the acre to sell by the foot, he is fraudulent, he is malefactor, so far; & is bringing society to bankruptcy. But nature watches over all this too, & turns this malfaisance to some good. For, California gets peopled, subdued, civilised, in this fictitious way, & on this fiction a real prosperity is rooted and grown.

Needless to say, this book is Emersonian in its orientation; I suppose that it is Milton Friedman, of all people, who is the modern inheritor of Thoreau.

Very often, the villain one blames for rising prices has to do with one's relation to the product in question. David Halberstam quite clearly thinks that it is producers who have "inflated" basketball salaries. But when it comes to the big journalistic books he writes, he is certain (with some justice, I think) that he has created a new and superior product (the "New Journalism") and that it is worth the higher price we pay for it.

Obviously, there is an intricate dialectic between money and complexity. Franklin Spinney, the defense analyst, is eloquent when he describes how defense project officers purposely omit from their estimates the costs of airplane operation and maintenance in the expectation that the next round of congressional appropriations will bail them out. In the same way, the existence of various sorts of medical insurance skewed toward "shallow" coverage has undoubtedly fostered different sorts of hypercomplexity, in the form of unnecessary procedures and admissions, in for-profit and nonprofit hospitals. Then, too, the difficulty of identifying the key person in the purchase of complex systems is notorious. Salesmen realize that it is crucial to know who in a complex organization makes the decision to purchase a given good or service, and what it is this person really wants; they know how difficult this is to determine.

For this reason, I think it is as misleading to say "complexity causes money" as it is to say "money causes complexity." The two always go hand in hand. As Martin Buber said of sex, so it is with supply and demand, money and complexity: they are an unfathomably intricate mix of monologue and dialogue.

ADDING IT UP

I hope that by now I have demonstrated satisfactorily that the "general price level," as measured by, for example, the CPI, is at least to some degree a function of the complexity of the number of different parts in the system. In the health care, defense, energy, and basketball sectors of the economy, consumers are not simply paying "a lot more money for the same old thing." Instead, they are getting a new and more complicated bundle of goods and services for their money. The higher prices reflect a new and more complex division of labor.

So what? Is this process merely a different type of "inflation," as Martin Feldstein thought? Is it another little wrinkle for the textbooks to record? If so, then econometricians can put a term for complexity in their big mathematical models and forget about it. They can add a new subheading—"complexity inflation" or "quality change inflation"—to "cost-push inflation" and "demand-pull inflation" and file it away; journalists can write semiannual stories about its neglected effects. But we should not stop there, and for this simple reason. What we know now is that the problem in medicine, in defense, in oil, and in government is not "too much money chasing too few goods," as the Quantity Theory of Money would suggest. If we are to understand modern markets—and why the cost of living has been rising without interruption since the eve of World War II—we need a new conceptual framework that permits us to see money *and* complexity, a unified and general way of thinking about the changing world of work.

4

THE COMPLEXITY
HYPOTHESIS I

A $10 BILL USED TO BE A LOT OF MONEY. EVERYBODY HAS A FA-
vorite story of what it meant to have one before World War II.
Then, $10 would buy a shirt, a bag of groceries, and a hardcover
book, and you would still have change left over. It would buy
three days at a seaside inn on Martha's Vineyard with three
meals a day. It was a week's rent for an apartment on East Fif-
ty-seventh Street in New York City.

Today, however, $10 doesn't go far. Shirt prices have
climbed to $25 from $5, beefsteak prices to $5 from 49 cents a
pound, book prices to a minimum of $15 from $3, hotel prices
to $75 from $3 a day, and two-bedroom apartment rents in New
York to more than $1,000 from less than $50 a month. A newspaper that used to cost 2 cents now costs a quarter.

This is usually called "inflation," and though it has been going on for fifty years, there is still no general agreement on why
it is happening or what it means. Few problems have been more
puzzling or deeply interesting to such a wide variety of people
than the tendency of prices to rise year after year since the end
of World War II.

What is there to say generally about the reasons for the change in the purchasing power of money?

THE LONG VIEW

First, it is important to know precisely what has happened to what we loosely call the cost of living. How much has it gone up? How different are the prices we pay for everyday goods today from what they were in the past? Anecdote is all very well, but what do the systematic measures say?

To begin with, economists don't often seek to measure the cost of living in a specific way. It is too hard, they say, to allow for the myriad changes in a family's budget. Instead, price historians concentrate on measuring simpler "market baskets" such as the consumer price index or a wholesale price index or some other particular collection of goods and services that are typical of the needs of a wide class of people. The markets measure the "price level," as it is called, or its inverse, "the purchasing power of money." When prices are up, "purchasing power" is down. There is no one particular or "correct" price level for a particular time or place; instead, there are many levels, depending on whose buying habits the shopping basket is based on. But though some are volatile and others are sluggish, most price levels tend to move together, and it is the "general" price level, which is an abstraction that is their average, that is of interest.

This "general price level" in America has for more than two hundred years fluctuated around a mean, increasing sharply with wars, decreasing sharply again with peace, and rarely standing higher at the end of a century than at the beginning. The history of prices thus told vaguely resembles a fever chart with a series of abrupt spikes rising from the plane of "normal"; it is in such a spike, beginning in about 1939, that we now find ourselves—"the Great Inflation," as the economist Robert Heilbroner has called it.

Two representative specimens of this conventional sort of price history—one for America and one for England—are worth a look. The American example, which may be found in Figure 5, is the CPI, charted in the course of one hundred and eighty years. The index is a creation of the Bureau of Labor Statistics, which keeps track of official government price statistics like the CPI; the years from 1800 to 1914 are estimates, made to resolve arguments about the cost of living that arose during World War I. This long-term CPI shows the price of a more or less unchanging basket of goods and services required for everyday life, such as food, shelter, transportation, and health care. Its general shape is clear: prices soar during wartime and fall afterward, but rarely to their prewar lows. The continuity is startling: on the eve of World War II, the purchasing power of the dollar, as measured by the CPI, was about what it had been before the American Revolution. After World War II, the Great Inflation set in and hasn't yet ended.

In the English case, which can be found in Figure 6, the mor-

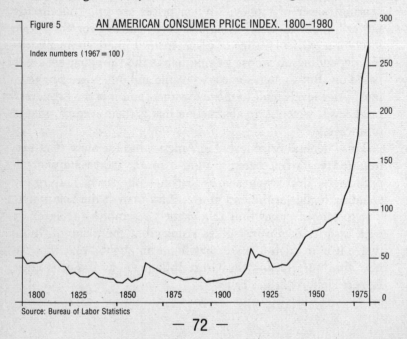

Figure 5   AN AMERICAN CONSUMER PRICE INDEX. 1800–1980

Index numbers (1967 = 100)

Source: Bureau of Labor Statistics

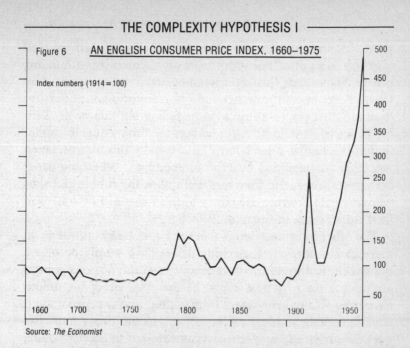

Figure 6 AN ENGLISH CONSUMER PRICE INDEX, 1660–1975

Index numbers (1914 = 100)

Source: *The Economist*

al about the purchasing power of money is similar and even more striking: money's value has historically been relatively stable, with prices rising in one year and falling the next, rarely going in either direction for more than a few years in a row. The price level whose measurement is displayed is of a series of market baskets stretching back some three hundred years; it was assembled by the magazine *The Economist* and is often exhibited to illustrate the conviction that the cost of living was little different in 1934 from what it had been in 1661, the year of the Restoration. In England, as in the United States, sharp spikes in the price level are associated with wars: the Napoleonic Wars particularly stand out. Again, the modern experience represents a striking departure from past experience: rather than falling after World War II, prices have been climbing ever since.

Arising from these data are two quite different schools of thought about what the Great Inflation of the last forty years portends. One interpretation is that the modern episode is just another fever spike, an especially dramatic one associated with

— 73 —

the Cold War, and that it will eventually burn itself out and give way to a great "postwar" depression, complete with falling prices. Sometimes this interpretation has been given a somewhat cheery spin; the writer for *The Economist* concludes, for example, that prices would soon be falling but that no slackening of activity would be required because "the sequel to slumpflation is a falling price boom." But usually this interpretation has been accompanied by grim foreboding ("When the paper system collapses, the survivors will dig in the rubble and they will find gold," wrote the editor of the *Times* of London, William Rees-Mogg, in the mid-1970s).

The other interpretation is that the Great Inflation will go on more or less forever, that rising prices have simply become a permanent feature of life in the modern world. Various reasons are offered for why this should be the case: either big unions have been able to keep wages from falling, or giant corporations have been able to keep prices up, or, in the thesis most frequently advanced, modern governments are no longer willing or able to tolerate sufficiently high levels of unemployment to achieve price stability. The conclusion is always the same: the purchasing power of money may have been more or less stable in the past, but it isn't anymore. Remember, despite a slump of as great a depth and duration as the 1980–82 recession, the "inflation" rate remains at approximately 5 percent a year.

If we pull back a little further, however, to take a still longer view of the history of prices and pay a little more attention to the yardstick we use, the situation changes dramatically. The graph in Figure 7 is the seven-hundred-year price index that I mentioned in the Introduction, taken from a 1956 issue of the British journal *Economica*. Showing what has happened to the money price of a more or less unchanging basket of consumables over the course of seven centuries, it was compiled by a professor at the London School of Economics named Sir Henry Phelps Brown and his assistant Sheila V. Hopkins. Phelps Brown and Hopkins also made a long-term record of the aver-

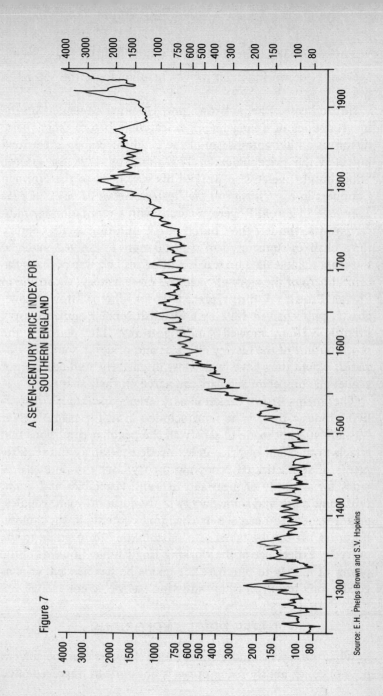

Figure 7

A SEVEN-CENTURY PRICE INDEX FOR
SOUTHERN ENGLAND

Source: E.H. Phelps Brown and S.V. Hopkins

age wages of workingmen to which to compare the record of prices.

In each case, Phelps Brown and Hopkins depended on the investigations of a long line of researchers before them. Price history is an old enthusiasm of the English: Bishop Fleetwood invented the price index in 1707, and by 1798 Sir George Shuckburgh-Evelyn had worked his way back to the Norman Conquest in his *Estimate of the Depreciation of Money Since the Year 1050*. Thorold Rogers, a curate with a reputation for radical politics who left the Church in the mid-nineteenth century for a chair in statistics, had painstakingly assembled much of the most reliable data on wages and prices and was perhaps the central hero of the story of wage and price history, according to Phelps Brown. A direct precedent for Phelps Brown's own charts, published in 1892 by a Swedish scholar named Gustav Fredrik Steffan, showed similar features. The point is, the broad outline of the history of wages and prices in southern England, where they have been most intensively studied, are not vague; all competent scholars can agree on their shape.

The Phelps Brown basket is not, strictly speaking, a cost-of-living index—there is no rent included in it, for example. Nor was any attempt made to satisfy all the peculiar conditions that attach to the kind of price index needed to satisfy the requirements of sophisticated economic theory. But the bundle provides for a supply of meat and fish and vegetables and grain, plus some cloth and some energy in the form of wood, candles, or kerosene. (You can see its changing contents in the table in Figure 8.) It can be taken as a reliable long-term guide to the everyday experience of the working Englishman in terms of the power of money to purchase the goods he has needed. It is as good a long-term record of "inflation" as we've got.

THREE PRICE EXPLOSIONS

What the seven-hundred-year index shows is that the current bout of continuously rising prices is not quite as unprecedented as it might seem, at least to those with shorter memories or more elaborate measuring instruments. By comparison to the series of ups and downs of the more short-term indexes, the Phelps Brown index in Figure 7 looks like a cross section of a set of steps dug into a hillside. Big explosions in the cost of living have taken place twice previously in the seven-hundred-year span of the index, once in the sixteenth century and once in the eighteenth century. Indeed, historians often have described these bursts of unremitting and unreversed "inflation" as "price explosions." These explosions are most remarkable occurrences. They start, go on for decades, and then stop. At their end, the purchasing power of money has declined sharply, never to increase again.

Between the eras of continuously rising prices, however, the cost of living has remained stable for periods of a century or more, fluctuating around a certain level: up a little one year, down the next, but within a relatively narrow range. The result is that no single person's experience with "inflation" is a very reliable guide to what comes next. If you happened to be born in 1640, for example, the value of the pound sterling would have been essentially the same for you, your children, and your grandchildren. If you were born in 1740, on the other hand, you would have lived your whole life in a time of rising prices, and the advice you would have given your grandchildren would probably have been quite worthless, since their century, the nineteenth, was an age of slowly *declining* prices.

Why is it that the Phelps Brown data exhibit a "price explosion" in England in the eighteenth century—a rough doubling of the price of the basket of goods—whereas the accounts in Figure 6 and many other indexes show no such thing? Tentatively, the answer seems to be that the Phelps Brown index measures the price of a simple and fundamentally unchanging basket of goods, whereas other indexes take far greater pains to make their samples conform to the dictates of economic theory, including taking account of substitutions they believe that consumers might make in response to rising prices. (When the

APPROXIMATE QUANTITIES OF ARTICLES MAKING UP THE COMPOSITE UNIT
OF CONSUMABLES, AROUND FOUR DATES

	1275	1500	1725	1950
1. Farinaceous	1¼ bush. wheat 1 bush. rye ½ bush. barley ⅔ bush. peas	1¼ bush. wheat 1 bush. rye ½ bush. barley ⅔ bush. peas	1½ bush. wheat ¾ bush. rye ⅓ bush. barley ½ bush. peas	2 bush. wheat 1 cwt. potatoes
2. Meat, fish	The meat of ½ pig ½ sheep 40 herrings	The meat of 1½ sheep 15 white herrings 25 red herrings	The meat of ½ sheep 33 lb. beef 1¼ salt cod	The meat of ⅔ sheep 28 lb. beef 1½ lb. cod 3 lb. herrings
3. Butter, cheese	10 lb. butter 10 lb. cheese	nil	10 lb. butter 10 lb. cheese	10 lb. butter 10 lb. cheese
4. Drink	4½ bush. malt	4½ bush. malt	3¼ bush. malt 3 lb. hops 1½ lb. sugar	2⅓ bush. malt 2¼ lb. hops 5 lb. sugar 4½ lb. tea
5. Fuel, light	nil	4¼ bush. charcoal 2¾ lb. candles ½ pt. oil	1½ bush. charcoal 1 cwt. coal 2½ lb. candles ½ pt. oil	2 cwt. coal 5½ pts. paraffin 300 cu. ft. coal gas
6. Textiles	3¼ yd. canvas	⅔ yd. canvas ½ yd. shirting ⅛ yd. woollen cloth	½ yd. woollen cloth	¾ lb. wool yarn 3 yds. printer's cotton cloth

Figure 8

price of meat soars, people stop buying meat and buy more bread.) I have no wish to argue with the fundamental insights of index number theory, but I fear that the more sophisticated accounts filter out the very event in which we are interested, a sustained and unreversed "inflation" of the basic price level in the years between 1760 and 1815. The Phelps Brown data are a remarkably "pure" price history, about as free from the coloration of theoretical expectation as possible.

Much scholarly research confirms the existence of a third unreversed "inflation"—what Lord Beveridge has called "the price explosion of the Middle Ages"—that ended in the twelfth century, just before the seven-hundred-year index begins. Again, the dating and magnitude of the explosion vary greatly with the location and the analyst. Again, however, the unreversed character of the explosion is of great interest. "Prices of all agricultural products rose suddenly and sharply in the closing years of the twelfth and the opening years of the thirteenth centuries," writes M. M. Postan in *The Medieval Economy and Society: An Economic History of Britain in the Middle Ages*. "Having risen to their turn-of-the-century plateau," he continues, "prices stayed on or above it for the rest of the thirteenth and early fourteenth centuries." Other investigations show the upward trend of prices continuing through most of the thirteenth century before giving way to generally stable prices at just about the time the Phelps Brown index begins.

It should be said that in comparison to our own twentieth-century price explosion, these three earlier events were rather mild affairs. The cost of living may have quickly doubled during the price explosion of the Middle Ages and then drifted slightly upward for years. The price of Phelps Brown and Hopkins's composite bundle increased about tenfold in the sixteenth century; other estimates put the increase of the English cost of living at around sixfold. The eighteenth-century price revolution saw the cost of the Phelps Brown bundle double and perhaps rise even a little more than this; other price indexes for the period show that the cost of living in certain ways climbed still more than this, and in other ways, less. By contrast, the increase in prices that set in around 1890 had reached a fourfold level by 1954, the year the Phelps Brown index stopped, and the rate of increase has been even more rapid since then, with perhaps as much as a tenfold or greater rise in prices.

What the series doesn't show are the remarkable changes in relative prices that have taken place over the years. In the introduction to his 1939 study of *Prices and Wages in England from the Twelfth to the Nineteenth Century*, Lord Beveridge noted that before the Black Death, at Hinderclay in Suffolk, a quarter (bushel) of wheat cost around 5 shillings, while steel for plowshares and other implements cost around 50 pounds sterling per ton. Six hundred years later, Beveridge said, wheat cost 50 shillings a quarter while steel cost about 10 pounds sterling a ton. In other words, a quarter of wheat would buy about fifty times as much steel as it once did. "The contrast between the wheat age and the steel age could hardly be better illustrated." Fascinating—but such exchange ratios are not the topic under consideration here.

What the seven-hundred-year price index provides is a good guide to what the average worker must have experienced as his cost of living. It is true that the intricacies of English price history are great; true that the very meaning of a shilling changed remarkably over the years. (The use of the term "shilling" in the new English decimal currency is now mostly a formality; it is more likely you will be asked for ten pence rather than for two shillings.) And it is true also that the Phelps Brown data were taken largely from college account books, in which long-term contracts provided some shelter from the wild gyrations of day-to-day prices in the marketplace. But the broad shape of the story simply is not in doubt. For a hundred years or more, the purchasing power of money will scarcely change at all, after which prices suddenly will start to climb and will keep rising, year after year, until it seems that they will go on climbing forever. Then, as quickly as it began climbing, the cost of living will level off on a new plateau, and the purchasing power of money will be relatively stable once again.

The Phelps Brown index thus poses vivid questions about current tendencies in the cost of living. Will prices fall back to their previous levels in a great crash? Or will they go on rising forever? Or, as has happened three times in the past, will they level off on a new plateau? Above all, why does the history of the cost of living in England take the shape it does? What was happening in those earlier episodes of price explosion that is also happening now? Like the rings of a tree, the Phelps Brown numbers serve to illuminate our understanding of economic history.

HEDGEHOGS VERSUS FOXES

The long episode of rising prices that began with World War II has most often been explained by stating that "the money supply" has been increasing faster than the supply of goods and services. The bankers of the Federal Reserve System in the United States, and of virtually every other industrial nation's central bank, have permitted money to grow faster than output, either because they are foolish, malicious, or simply cowardly—so the argument goes. In any event, the value of the dollar has declined because too many dollars have been printed.

This is, of course, the Quantity Theory of Money, which contributes the word "inflation" to our vocabulary and provides most of the apparatus with which we analyze the phenomenon it describes. The Quantity Theory holds that the price of a typical basket of goods—the behavior of a price index, in other words—is a matter of the proportion between money and things. If the money supply has been allowed to increase more rapidly than the goods and services of the world, according to the Quantity Theory, the result is that prices go up. "Inflation" is therefore "too much money chasing too few goods."

The great strength of the Quantity Theory is that it has so much to say about the episodes of price explosion reflected in the Phelps Brown numbers. Indeed, the Quantity Theory may be said to have been invented in the second half of the sixteenth century to account for that long period of "inflation," for a connection between New World treasure and rising prices was often noted then. (A contemporary writer, Marc Lescabot, complains, "Before the voyages to Peru, one could keep much wealth in a little place, but now that gold and silver have been cheapened by abundance, great chests are required to transport what before could be carried wrapped up in a piece of drugget. A man could go a long way with a purse up his sleeve, but now he needs a trunk and a horse.'') In the eighteenth century, also, monetary disturbance was again found to be the source of rising prices; this time it was the spread of paper money and commercial credit that was thought to be the cause. Great controversies raged among learned men as pound notes replaced coins; they have a curiously modern sound. David Ricardo writes that ''however abundant may be the quantity of money or of banknotes; though it may increase the nominal prices of commodities; though it may distribute the productive capital in different proportions . . . nothing will be added to the real revenue and wealth of the country. . . . There will be a violent and unjust transfer of property, but no benefit whatever will be gained by the community.'' And in the twentieth century the Quantity Theory again identifies a handy villain: the source of the disturbance in the quantity of money in our century is thought by many people to be some sort of unholy alliance among fractional banking, the Federal Reserve System, and government, which ''prints money'' to finance its activities. ''If you want to analyze the process of inflation,'' says Milton Friedman, *cherchez la monnaie*.''

Nevertheless, many thoughtful persons, from the eighteenth century on, have considered that an increasing supply of money is a necessary but not sufficient condition for rising prices, that ''something else'' drives the spiral, and that the supply of money passively responds to such ''other'' forces. ''Fix any M1 and the market will create new forms of money in periods of boom to get around the limit and create the necessity to fix a new variable, M2'' is the way Charles Kindleberger put it. Napoleon, bad weather, and new methods of manufacturing were some of the causes cited by contemporaries of the eighteenth-century price explosion—bills and banknotes and other new forms of credit simply arose to finance the required expansion of trade. Big unions, bad companies, greedy Arabs, high taxes, and the shift to a service economy are some of the reasons cited for the ''wage-price spiral'' of the postwar years—bank lending and government borrowing were required to accommodate them.

Of course, no two analysts can agree on exactly what factors are to blame, and nobody can locate precisely similar factors at work in earlier times.

This is the real rub. The "nonmonetarist" dissidents make up the majority of serious students of "inflation." They include many celebrated economists, such as the late Joan Robinson and Otto Eckstein, as well as Robert Solow, John Kenneth Galbraith, Lester Thurow, Nicholas Kaldor, Charles Kindleberger, and Robert Heilbroner. These "nonmonetarists" can be eloquent (Heilbroner), acerbic (Robinson), amusing (Galbraith), and technically proficient (Eckstein), yet they rarely define with any real generality the identity of this "something else" behind "inflation." So "nonmonetarism" really adds up to the widely shared sense that "a lot of little things" are at work in causing "inflation." In the ancient Greek distinction revived by Sir Isaiah Berlin, "nonmonetarists" are "foxes," who see many things, while monetarists are "hedgehogs," who see one big thing.

The power of the Quantity Theory to dominate discussion is very great, however. For example, with its eleventh edition in 1980, Paul Samuelson's famous introductory textbook entitled *Economics* began for the first time to include a graphic representation of the Phelps Brown index. Significantly, Samuelson accepted the monetarist explanation for the price explosions of the sixteenth and eighteenth centuries while implicitly rejecting it for the twentieth-century episode. "Price inflation has dogged the history of capitalism," he writes, adding that "the rise in money supply from New World silver and gold, and from the Napoleonic War printing of paper money [has] associated with it the rise in prices."

There have been only two major attempts to supplant the Quantity Theory in this century. John Maynard Keynes was the author of the first; he describes his *General Theory of Money, Employment and Interest* as his "final escape" from "the confusions of the Quantity Theory." A fascinating story is how Milton Friedman caught him with an effective reformulation of the Quantity Theory and brought him back. Sidney Weintraub wasn't so lucky. Trembling with excitement, he published, in 1959, a little book called *A General Theory of the Price Level, Output, Income Distribution and Economic Growth* after a whirlwind writing stint. He sought to substitute the concept of K, a constant markup of prices over wages paid, for the concept of M, the money supply. He compared K to the universal gravitation constant. It wasn't mentioned in his obituary when he died in 1983.

The result is that, in the absence of a truly general alternative explanation, elementary economics textbooks still serve up the Quantity Theory in their introductory chapters—in order to disagree with it later in the judgmental sections in which theory is tempered with common sense. Paul Samuelson's book is typical. "Rudimentary as it is, then, the crude Quantity Theory linking P (the price level) directly to M (the quantity of money) is useful to describe periods of hyperinflation and various long-term trends in prices, such as those in Spain and elsewhere in Europe after New World treasure was discovered," writes Samuelson. Robert Heilbroner says more or less the same. So does John Kenneth Galbraith. Yet despite their valiant attempts to escape, the "nonmonetarists" are captives of the Quantity Theory's analytic framework; it is a language, and they are its prisoners, no matter which dialect they speak.

AN ALTERNATIVE FRAMEWORK

Without being unfair, we may, I think, compare the monetarist interpretation of "inflation" to the theory of a flat earth. That is, it carries a lot more intellectual baggage with it than first meets the eye. For example, unless you've already got the idea of a round earth firmly in mind, speaking of "the far corners" seems perfectly harmless; likewise, you still struggle to come up with a convincing theory to explain the concept of "edge." Even if you weren't comfortable with the policy implications of flat-earthism ("Don't sail West!" among them), it wouldn't do you much good to profess "nonflat" theories of the earth. You can't leave such a big and necessary idea unless you've got someplace else to go.

Such a "place to go" from the Quantity Theory begins with the idea of economic complexity. By complexity, as stated in the Introduction, I mean the number of different kinds of jobs in an economy and the manner of their interconnection. I shall now make the proposition that the cost of living, as well as the quantity of money, is a function of the complexity of the system; that a continually rising price index probably means not that you're getting nothing more for your money but rather that you are buying a new and more complicated product. I call this the "complexity hypothesis." As we shall see, it is not a theory of "inflation" at all. Crude as it is, the complexity hypothesis may offer an alternative to the Quantity Theory of Money.

Certainly the complexity hypothesis offers a quite different account of why prices have been rising since World War II, one far more consonant with the answers usually given for this increase than the money supply explanation. All of the "special factors" and "little things" that are usually mentioned in connection with rising prices—everything from government regulation to administered prices to pushy unions—can be dealt with in terms of growing complexity. Not that it will be easy: much work lies ahead in distinguishing between different kinds of complexity and learning to measure them, just as tiresome debates over money have been going on for two centuries. But it is work that will be rewarded with a clearer picture of the world.

Complexity is rarely a day-to-day force. It is a secular factor, a long-term force, an aspect of the deep structure of the organization of human society.

DO WE NEED IT?

I emphatically do not mean to blame everything that has to do with rising (or falling) prices on complexity. Nor does the idea of complexity suggest a theory for the value of things: there is no implication here that an avocado costs more than a potato because it is more complex. In this deeply complicated world, complexity is but one small tool for organizing our experience. So is the concept of the quantity of money.

What I find most difficult in propounding these matters is persuading people that these two notions, money and complexity, are not simply two different factors that must both be weighed in the balance but that they instead represent two conflicting interpretations of experience that are mutually exclusive, at least in some situations, and that one must ultimately be preferred to the other. Most people will quickly cede some role in rising prices to burgeoning complexity. And they will also observe that the ease of monetary accommodation has something to do with the process. What they won't do readily is stand back and examine the origins of the framework with which we talk about these matters. They want to know, "Why not be eclectic?" Obviously a great many diverse factors influence the consumer price index, including bad harvests and the rate of growth of the money supply. Why be stubborn about attributing it all to complexity? Why not just put a complexity term in the big econometric models and forget it?

I would be perfectly content to be eclectic if we were not already gripped by a Big Idea with which we classify our economic experience, for the most part unconsciously. I mean, of course, the Quantity Theory of Money, which, in response to the question "What is the meaning of generally rising prices?" gives us an answer masquerading as a description in the form of the word "inflation." We say, "What is the cause of 'inflation'?" or "What are the components of 'inflation'?" or "What is the best policy against 'inflation'?" and however eclectic we are determined to be, we are predisposed to certain conclusions by the way we put the question. This is like trying to be eclectic while answering the question "Where is the edge of the earth?"

It is my contention that both the Quantity Theory (and the

whole wide range of monetarist interpretations that it engenders) and the complexity hypothesis are "ways of seeing" the same process of rising prices. They arise from different metaphoric foundations, if you like, and I think that they are fundamentally incompatible. Over the years, I have learned to depend on a number of rhetorical devices to drive this point home. For example, I tend to make a good deal of the Phelps Brown numbers, whose shape this chapter has set out to explain, because they pose the question with special clarity. Sometimes, as in the Introduction, I ask readers to reflect on the factors that determine the purchasing power of money in restaurants, noting that the difference in lunch prices at a plain eatery and at its fancy counterpart owes not to the disparity in the quantity of money in each but rather to the difference in complexity.

But for the present purpose, perhaps I can best illustrate the relationship among complexity, prices, and money by resorting to a well-known game. This game doesn't tell us very *much* about the way the world works, but it does cast a bright light on one aspect of it. It has achieved nearly universal assent, if not forthright recognition, as a model of the changing cost of living. Consider, if you will, the Darrow model.

THE DARROW MODEL

Charles Darrow has been much lionized as a heating engineer who, as a victim of the Great Depression, devised a simple board game to remind him of the happier days he had spent in Atlantic City; he then sold it to Parker Brothers and reaped a fortune. As Parker Brothers' Monopoly, the game is played all over the world. It turns out that Darrow was a ne'er-do-well who stole the game from a group of Quakers who taught it to him; it had been invented thirty years before by followers of Henry George, who created it to illustrate "single tax" principles. All this has been brought to light in the most interesting way by a remarkable historian of economic thought named Ralph Anspach, who is telling his own story in another book that has yet to be published. The point is the game itself.

As nearly everyone knows, Monopoly is played on a board patterned after the street layout of Atlantic City. Players get a token and $1,500 apiece, then take turns throwing the dice and moving their tokens around the board, buying up land and developing it. The throw of dice governs the flow of the game. The relative prices of land are static—$260 to buy Ventnor Avenue, $350 for the Boardwalk—and like almost everything else in the game, they are dictated by deeds. There are no formal auctions and few informal ones. The "general price level," as opposed to the relative price system, is the average rent. The "cost of landing" on owned properties is the game's proxy for the cost of living.

At first rents are low, and a little money goes a long way. It costs $2 for a stop on Mediterranean Avenue, $16 if you land on New York Avenue. And so at its beginning the game is played largely with $1 and $5 bills.

As the game unfolds, however, prices climb. By the time the players have assembled "color blocs," the monopoly groupings of property necessary to begin the next stage of the game, it costs $44 for a stop on Ventnor Avenue—its rent has doubled with the formation of the monopoly, according to the deed. Houses are built, then hotels. Players pay for the development of their properties with their cash, then recoup their investments through higher rents. The cost of landing on nearly every square escalates sharply; on Ventnor Avenue rent climbs to $110, $330, $800, $975, and finally to $1,150.

In a short time, the $1 bills with which the game began are nearly worthless (and are scarcely used). Instead, $50s, $100s, and $500s are the rule. At the end of the game, the average cost of landing on a deeded property—our proxy for the general price level—has risen to $950 from $18 at the beginning. There isn't enough money in the players' hands to continue. The game ends amid falling prices in a contrived liquidity crunch.

In other words, by the end of the game the price level has climbed—indeed, exploded—while the purchasing power of money has shrunk. But who thinks of Monopoly as a game of "inflation"? Who would say that the rising cost of landing was a matter of "too much money chasing too few properties"? Who waxes nostalgic about the passing of the usefulness of the $1 bill?

It is true that the quantity of money increases throughout the game, rising by $200 every time a player passes Go. Indeed, at the end of the game, the money supply is more than twice what it was at the beginning. It is also true that if the money supply didn't increase, the rents couldn't very well go up and there would be no "inflation." But how long would a banker who refused to dole out those $200 increments to Go-passers last in his job?

Yet does increasing money "cause" the rising prices in Monopoly? Of course not. It is the construction of houses and hotels—the costs of development—that in the logic of the game are the real reasons for the rising prices. Players take it for granted that prices will rise, that money will "decline in its value," as the game goes along because they know that Monopoly is a game of increasing complexity. What happens is the "goldplating" of the board; when you pay $1,300 in rent for landing on Park Place with four houses on it, it is not that you are getting nothing more for your money; you are spending it instead on a different product in a more complex system.

The original, pre-Darrow Monopoly game was devised to deal with post-gold-rush California, but it has a certain universality. It leaves out much, but it includes the factors that make the difference in determining price levels. Anytime you wonder about the fate of the English shilling, which bought so much before World War II, think of Monopoly and the fate of a $1 bill.

There is a second service that the Darrow model can render. It can serve as a kind of dressmaker's dummy while we try to fashion a garment—our vocabulary for describing the real world. If we can come up with terms to describe our intuitive sense of what happens in Monopoly, we'll have a basis for talking with greater clarity about economic reality.

THE DIFFUSION OF COSTS

How shall we describe what happens to prices in a world in which economic complexity, rather than the supply of money, is seen to be the dominant factor? If "inflation" doesn't describe the process, what word will?

The process that is at the center of rising prices in the real world is the "passing on" and "folding in" of new costs that are incurred as complexity increases. It is this that Monopoly captures and takes for granted. The price of the OPEC price hike, for example, is "passed on" by the oil companies and "folded into" the price of a gallon of gas, as we have already noted. Similarly, the price of a new CAT scanner is "folded into" the price of a hospital bed and "passed on" to patients and their insurance companies. It makes sense to call this passing-on process the "diffusion" of costs, meaning their spread from an area of high concentration to ever wider areas of lower concentration.

Diffusion has a clear meaning, originally derived from chemistry; thus, a single drop of brilliant purple iodine that is placed in a glass of water diffuses until all the water in the glass is tinted a pale lavender. The word has a range of equally clear and similar meanings in the social sciences. We routinely speak of the diffusion of technologies from their point of introduction, for example, of the diffusion of influence and of the diffusion of style. Why not the diffusion of the costs? It is a far more concrete and potentially measurable process, after all.

Diffusion has the advantage of combining, under a single heading, a number of gerunds that have second-class standing in economics but that nevertheless perform heavy descriptive duty in the everyday language of the trade. I am speaking of words such as "shifting," "pushing," "exporting," and "passing on" of costs as well as "flowing through," "percolating down," and any number of even less specific terms used to describe the way that cost increases are passed from one supplier to manufacturer to consumer and back again. As matters stand, the particular gerund we choose depends upon the kind of cost we are talking about. In this regard, we are rather like the South American Indians who have five hundred words with different shades of meaning for describing the color of a horse. Yet we never make any attempt to add up the effects of these various processes. Diffusion provides a convenient filing cabinet in which to place all these kinds of cost, in order to see the process whole.

In fact, the word "diffusion" had just this meaning in the nineteenth century, especially when applied to taxes, but its use was relentlessly challenged by the early pioneers of what has since come to be known as "incidence theory," and with good reason. In economics, the act of passing on is a moment without any great significance, a fleeting step in the transition from one equilibrium point to another. The familiar tripartite division of costs into labor, capital, and raw materials leaves no place for the kind of adding up I am describing. A sudden shock in the form of higher oil prices, for example, will be seen simply as a matter of relative price change. Capital will be more expensive relative to labor—or the other way around. If there is a little more stress on one ingredient in the system, there is a little less stress on another, somewhere, somehow. Or so the argument goes.

Diffusion, on the other hand, takes the talk out of the realm of the one-time event. "Pushing" is no longer something that I do to you if I can, once and for all, as if I were rearranging the furniture of a room. Instead, it becomes something that everyone does to everyone else, all of the time, whenever there is a new cost to be borne. "Cumulative shifting" is about as close as conventional economic vocabularies now come to this dynamic sense of the word. Cumulative shifting and not "inflation" is what the "cost-push" or "wage-price spiral" argument is all about.

More important, however, the use of the word "diffusion" takes the process of rising prices out of the realm of the timeless and locates it firmly in history. We speak of the diffusion of *new* costs causing increases in *old* prices. Every item and event in the world get a time subscript even in the most casual language: for example, we might say of Monopoly that with the diffusion of house prices, the cost of landing rose. There is no place in the Quantity Theory for this kind of talk. Instead, there is only the "inflation" of *all* prices—nothing new, nothing old.

I would think that the everyday evidence for the existence of diffusion is overwhelming. The only question concerns the magnitude of the force. One has only to think of the way in which rising health insurance costs are reflected in the CPI, then shifted into wages via cost-of-living-adjustment agreements, then shifted again into higher hospital prices through collective bargaining agreements. Whether it is a markup in sheet steel prices finding its way into the price of a shovel at Sears, an announced tax on the import of oil percolating through to the price of gas at the pump, or a new rise in the demand for copper rippling through the economy, the diffusion of costs is an everyday fact of economic life. It is just that there is not yet any measuring instrument with which to record its ebb and flow. Economists now handle it as a matter of the core or nonaccelerating rate of inflation and of "shocks" to it.

WHAT ARE WE MEASURING?

If the diffusion of the costs of added complexity is the cause of rising prices, then we cannot in fairness talk about the "inflation" of the prices we pay, for the word suggests that we are getting nothing more for our money. What then are our price indexes measuring if not "inflation"? Let me propose that we try speaking of the "conflation" of prices. The word is admirably suited to our purposes. It casts the unstated presupposition of the word "inflation" into sharp relief.

To conflate means to blend, to fuse, to add together. An old alchemical term, it is seldom heard these days outside scholarly circles, where it generally refers to something thought to be a sin ("You fool, you've conflated two different texts"). Yet conflation catches very nicely our sense of what actually happens to the price of a day in the hospital, for example, when an administrator adds a new ICU, meaning that the patient is buying a new and more complex mixture of products for his money. Is it stretching a point to talk of the conflation of oil prices through the development schemes of the oil-exporting countries? Perhaps, but it is a far more satisfactory description in terms of the overall economic system than is "inflation."

There may be nothing quite so difficult as altering the everyday language of economics. In the harder sciences, nomenclature changes frequently to reflect changes in the predominating conception. In introducing the terminological nightmare of *Das Kapital* to English readers, Marx's interpreter Frederick Engels himself pointed out that organic chemistry changed its descriptive apparatus every twenty years. But daily life does not have the self-confidently playful atmosphere of high science. It is all very well to talk of the "color" and "charm" of "quarks," but taxes and prices and profits are terms people take as seriously as their liberty.

It may be that the word "inflation" is here to stay. I certainly don't expect "conflation" to overwhelm it anytime soon. But the idea of conflation is useful even if it serves only to remind us what a loaded word we have when we use "inflation" to describe a rising price index. "Inflation" connotes a worldview no less interesting in its implications than the one we have in mind when we speak of the "edges" of the earth or the "transmutation" of the elements.

ECONOMIC REVOLUTIONS

Suppose we are asked to account for the causes of a spate of conflation? How would we describe what happened? How would we describe the way in which the economic world had changed? If we were talking about the Darrow model, wouldn't we talk about the "housing revolution"?

The word "revolution" is used in economics with no very great precision. Sometimes it means nothing more than a certain high rate of growth, a 3 percent or greater increase in the gross national product per capita. At other times the term is narrowed to mean any period of rapid technological change. Sometimes it is used to mean a change in the intellectual underpinnings of work amounting to a change in the rules of the game: "the scientific revolution." At still other times it means little more than a change in the kind of middlemen in a market: "the boxed beef revolution."

I propose that we use "revolution" to mean an increase in specialization and interdependence; in other words, an increase or at least a change in the complexity of the division of labor. Thus we can speak of "the industrial revolution," "the talkie revolution," "the paper copier revolution," "the managerial revolution," and even "the Darwinian revolution," and mean more or less the same thing: a change in the configuration of a community of workers. (Look for the Darwinian revolution in the organization of university departments of biology.) Revolutions almost always involve a change in technology; they *always* involve a change in the division of labor. A revolution is a significant change in the variety of niches in the economy. (A revolution doesn't always raise prices, but it almost always cuts costs—which, after all, is why it succeeds.)

Indeed, one might prefer a different word altogether. Gerhard Mensch, the German economist who is among the most original interpreters of the Kondratieff or "long wave" in economic affairs, has suggested the term "metamorphosis" in discussing the kinds of economic changes that we are calling revolutions. His aim is to get around the problem that is implicit generally in the cyclical analysis of economies.* The long-wave model distinguishes phases of boom and bust that are

---

* See Chapter 6 for a discussion of Kondratieff wave theorists.

simply repeated again and again, generating something like an uninterrupted sine wave, whereas the evidence of revolutionary changes in the extent of the division of labor suggests a series of S curves in which change speeds up and slows down and is cumulative.

Once again, it is precisely here, in its tendency to "add up" rather that "net out," that the complexity hypothesis differs from the more familiar cyclical point of view. Surely the important thing about specialization is its growth—sometimes fast, sometimes slow, but almost always in the direction of more specialization rather than less. The idea of metamorphosis captures this aspect of further growth and differentiation rather nicely. Nevertheless, I don't expect this term to catch on. "Revolution" seems here to stay. We should work, however, on what is meant by the word.

REVOLUTION? OR EVOLUTION?

Why should there be revolutions at all—why should change ever be quick and spasmodic rather than always slow and steady? This question was debated at length twenty years ago, after W. W. Rostow published *The Stages of Economic Growth,* a remarkable book in which he introduced the concept of economic "takeoff." In the resulting controversy over this "stage theory," talk of revolutionary versus evolutionary change was raised to a very high level by economists who chose sides. Needless to say, they didn't reach a conclusion, but they did leave a lengthening shelf of books on the subject—books that for the most part are ignored by today's econometricians, whose whole art depends on change being continuous.

Can we add anything to this debate? Perhaps. The nature of change is a matter of widespread debate in other fields, especially in the biological sciences. As Stephen Jay Gould puts it, the issue is: "Is our world . . . primarily one of constant change (with structure as a mere incarnation of the moment), or is structure primary and constraining, with change as a 'difficult' phenomenon, usually accomplished rapidly when a stable structure is stressed beyond its ability to resist and absorb?" The view expressed throughout this book is that economic change *is* "hard," in the sense that it occurs rapidly only when there are breakthroughs, usually in the stock of knowledge. If the growth of knowledge is, as it is nowadays often asserted to be, a matter of sharp shifts in viewpoint followed by long periods of "filling in the blanks," then nothing could be less surprising than that economic growth should also exhibit this "revolutionary" pattern. In any event, the structure of the Phelps Brown data, with its story of relative stability followed by sharp shifts, seems an important scrap of evidence to put in the balance on the side of the "punctuated equilibrium" view of life, at least in the case of rising prices. The shape of the history of prices speaks for itself.

Let the last word on the subject belong to a metallurgist at MIT. Cyril Stanley Smith is a man of astonishing breadth and depth. From his work in metals he developed an abiding interest in structure; in his long friendship with Lancelot Law Whyte he honed an equal interest in the history of innovation. In a series of essays collected in *A Search for Structure*, he stalks all around the idea of complexity. "Anything complex *must* have had a history, a sequence of changes in its parts," writes Smith. "A complex structure is a result of, and to a large extent a record of, its past. Though a proton and an electron may, as a pair, be able to spring full-panoplied from the head of Jove, more complex things certainly cannot, or at least do not."

Smith says that the "S curve" is "the shape of universal history," since all change that results from novelty is necessarily discontinuous. He explains:

A new thing of any kind whatsoever begins as a local anomaly, a region of misfit within the preexisting structure. The first nucleus is indistinguishable from the few fluctuations whose time has not yet come and the innumerable fluctuations which the future will merely erase. Once growth from an effective nucleus is well under way, however, it is then driven by the very type of interlock that at first opposed it: it has become the new orthodoxy. In crystals undergoing transformation, a region having an interaction pattern suggesting the new structure, once it is big enough, grows by demanding and rewarding conformity. With ideas or with technical or social inventions, people eventually come to accept the new as unthinkingly as they had at first opposed it, and they modify their lives, interactions and investments accordingly. But growth too has its limits. Eventually the new structure will have grown to its proper size in relation to the things with which it interacts, and a new balance must be established. The end of growth, like its beginning, is within a structure that is unpredictable in advance.

A better description of the process of economic growth is hard to find.

MEASURING COMPLEXITY

Diffusion, conflation, revolution: these are most of the concepts you need to know in order to think about the complexity hypothesis. One item is missing, however. If conflation of "the basic price level" is what we measure with a cost-of-living index, if increases in the money supply are what we measure with the monetary aggregates, and if the separation of the "core rate" from the effect of various "shocks" is the way we deal with diffusion, how do we measure complexity? What is a suitable metric for revolutions?

As noted, the basic tools for describing economic complexity are nothing other than the standard industrial classification (SIC) code and the occupational dictionary. In the Darrow model, we need only a very simple classification scheme that distinguishes between undeveloped lots, those already in monopoly blocs, houses, and hotels. We create it intuitively the second time we play Monopoly. In a world we do not understand so well, however, we need something far more complicated. The present SIC code sorts the American economy into nearly ten thousand industries. The occupational dictionary does the same thing for kinds of employment in firms.

Theory and measurement depend on each other; they cannot do without each other: but theory is clearly the senior partner. The complexity hypothesis requires the SIC code and a cost-of-living index in exactly the same way that the Quantity Theory requires the monetary aggregates and the price indexes. A theory with an indicator is impregnable; an indicator without a theory is a statistical orphan!

Yet a motherless child is precisely what the SIC code is. In these quickly changing times, an up-to-date basis for a census of industries would seem to be a matter of the first importance to economists and policymakers. A revision of the SIC code has been sitting on the shelf since 1980. A major revision hasn't been undertaken for ten years. Under orders from the Reagan administration, however, the revision remains unimplemented, and the further work that is necessary is waiting to be done. As a result, it is possible to describe with exquisite accuracy the composition of a textile industry that sometime in the 1960s all but ceased to exist in the United States, whereas virtually the entire computer industry is still lumped together in a single four-digit category.

An interesting glimpse of the way the SIC code is regarded by the Reagan administration was afforded in 1981, when I phoned the Office of Management and Budget in the course of preparing a story on the way the administration was "dimming the statistical lights" by which the economy was known. In a conversation with Edwin Dale, OMB's spokesman, and a former reporter for *The New York Times* and co-author of a fine elementary economics text, I suggested that the SIC code was a valuable tool that ought to be carefully maintained. Dale positively blustered at my remark. "SIC codes are not at all vital to macroeconomic policy," he said. "You'd need an SIC code—I mean, you have an SIC code, but a more refined one—if this country was going to have an industrial policy. . . . But this administration isn't about to have an industrial policy." When I called back in the fall of 1983, the revision was still being held up, ostensibly for budgetary reasons.

The same fate befell the Family Budget Series of the Bureau of Labor Statistics, a crude but interesting guide collected by the federal government to what I have been describing as "the basic price level." This cost-of-living indicator asked what after-tax income was necessary to purchase a particular basket of goods and services—or, rather, three different baskets, representing high, middle, and low standards of living. And it specified the contents of these baskets quite precisely—the kind of house, the kind of car, and the kinds of children's lunches.

Unfortunately, the "low" standard of living is irresistibly interesting to those concerned with the welfare of the poor. While it was collected, it was continually used to establish "the poverty line," and so ran afoul of legislators who, angry at the news that there were many who could be considered poor, finally killed the statistical messenger. Besides, the data were expensive to collect. Thus, the Family Budget Series was quietly discontinued by the Bureau of Labor Statistics during the Carter administration. The most interesting and valuable conflation indicator simply faded into the night.

HOW MONEY MATTERS

Contrast the treatment of the Family Budget Series with the loving attention paid to the monetary aggregates when they are released to a waiting world each Thursday afternoon. But then, why shouldn't this be so? The Quantity Theory and monetary controversy have developed hand-in-glove for two centuries, for as often as economists have reached the point at which they have thought they understood the process of money creation, prospectors and miners or bankers or credit managers have discovered new ways to create money. From the controversy between Banking and Currency Schools in England in the first half of the nineteenth century—over whether money was simply cash or credit also—right up to the present, there have been battles over which measure of total money supply is the most useful. After the Great Depression, in which the supply of money declined by more than a third in just a few years because of the failure of the banks, the Federal Reserve System set out to develop reliable indicators of the quantity of money in existence. The result is the richly articulated M set of indicators, ranging from from M1 (which includes only currency, checking accounts, traveler's checks, and demand deposits) through M2 (in which money market mutual fund shares, the overnight borrowing known as repurchase agreements or "repos," the dollar deposits in overseas banks known as "eurodollars," and small time deposits are added to M1), to M3 (in which large time deposits and term repos are added to M2), and L, the broad measure of all liquid assets that presumably includes everything from cereal coupons to bottle deposits.

Everyone who has ever taken a course in business and banking knows how banks create money. Clearly no one bank can create money—it can only lend a fraction of its deposits. But when banker A lends to customer A, customer A ordinarily spends immediately only a tiny portion of the money; the rest he deposits in bank B, creating deposits against which bank B can lend to customer B, who in turn deposits his cash in bank C, and so on. In this way money is created—about $5 in deposits on which checks can be written for every dollar of reserves.

It is through the regulation of these reserves that the central bank controls the money supply. Left to their own devices, bankers could probably get by in the best of times with very little money in the till—say, 2 percent of total deposits; as a precaution against bad times, when many customers want their money, governments require higher safety margins, usually between 10 and 20 percent. Higher reserve requirements mean there is less money in the system; lower reserves mean there will be more. But manipulating the reserve requirements is only the most coarse way by which the government pursues its monetary policies. It can influence the money supply more delicately by buying or selling government debt in the open market or by changing the discount rate—the interest rate it charges member banks who borrow sums of money for brief periods. The process of money creation is intricate and fascinating; there are many excellent books on the subject. The point is that the intricate mechanisms by which money is created and destroyed are well understood by experts. The fact that commercial bankers do not operate from duty—that when they lend money in the real world they make a profit—just complicates the issue.

The rules governing money creation, as opposed to the mechanisms, are another matter. In the game of Monopoly, the rules are simple: each player gets $1,500 to start and another $200 is injected each time a player passes Go. In the real world the rules are far more complicated. How do central bankers decide on their monetary targets? Do they lead the economy or do they react to it? Monetarists are adamant in their belief that it is incumbent upon central bankers to hold the line against "inflation" by keeping money growth steady.

But there is more to life than stable prices—unless, of course, you are a monetarist. Central bankers who "validate" or "accommodate" the various pressures in the real economy are simply playing by the generally accepted rules. Just as a Monopoly banker who refused to dole out $200 to players passing Go would quickly be sacked, so a central banker who refused to permit the money supply to increase roughly in line with economic activity would be fired. A fascinating testimony to this analysis was offered a few years ago by the man who taught Milton Friedman economics. Arthur Burns, who was chairman of the Federal Reserve System for a decade, said in a lecture in Belgrade in 1979, "Viewed in the abstract, the Federal Reserve System had the power to abort the inflation at its incipient stage fifteen years ago, or at any later point, and it has the power to end it today. At any time within that period, it could have restricted the money supply and created sufficient strains in financial and industrial markets to terminate inflation with little delay. It did not do so because the Federal Reserve itself was caught up in the philosophic and political currents that were transforming American life and culture."

So intimate is the dialectic between the supply of money and growth that it may be quite impossible to say that one causes the other. But it is possible to say that a hypothesis that discerns both growth in complexity and increase in the supply of money is cognitively superior to a hypothesis that discerns complexity alone. "Accommodation" describes the largely (but by no means entirely) passive role of the monetary authorities and commercial banks in the modern world.

CLIPPING CORNERS AND OTHER ARTIFICES

How does outright money-tinkering—that well-known fact of life—fit into the complexity hypothesis? Let me explain. The key is to recognize that when a government tampers with the money supply in certain well-understood and highly deliberate ways, it does so only because it is attempting to achieve some change in economic complexity. Money-tinkering will show up nearly as quickly in the SIC code as in the M figures.

Consider the possibilities. There are two main ways of getting people to do what you want them to do—of effecting and sustaining some particular change in the division of labor—and they correspond to two broad classes of cost designed to be imposed on one's fellow man. Either you can increase your profit, and pay for what you want done, or you can levy taxes—and pay for what you want done. Slavery was formerly an option; piracy and crime still are. But these are extreme cases. Taxes and prices are far and away the two most common ways of sustaining human enterprise. (I omit borrowing, to make things simple.)

However, it sometimes happens that clever persons resort to money-tinkering as a way of achieving their own goals. A king clips the corners off gold coins to pay his jugglers; a president sells a lot of government bonds to keep an army in the field; a counterfeiter runs off a batch of $100 bills. These tricks, which result in an increase in "the quantity of money" quite incidental to their goal, amount to a third way of financing an operation, and they can have a substantial impact on the general "purchasing power of money." There is no doubt whatsoever about this effect. From clipping coins to monetizing debt to manipulating reserve requirements, these measures raise the prices of most everything bought and sold.

Once again, the Darrow model illuminates the point, for the child who, as banker, deals himself an extra $100 or so from time to time is familiar to every player of Monopoly. But aside from giving him an unfair advantage, his money-tinkering serves only to speed up the pace of the game. It is only when he adds a house that the price level actually goes up. In the real world, one must recognize that it is the added complexity—the jugglers, the army, whatever—that represents the important factor in rising prices and not the extra money created to pay for them. Money-tinkering is the means, not the end. When Lyndon Johnson financed the war in Vietnam by technically "printing money," it was not the manipulation of the money that mattered, but rather a new wrinkle in the division of labor in American society—the army in Vietnam—that affected prices. The increase in the cost of living might have been somewhat less if the war had been financed by taxes—although prices still would have gone up had this been done.

WHAT ABOUT WEIMAR?

Monetarists are right to regard the "inflation of the money supply" as a tax. But they are wrong to think that other sorts of taxes have no effect on the cost of living. There are many excellent studies of governments using the power of the printing press to finance their activities, but whether it is the American Confederacy struggling to keep an army in the field or the government of the Weimar Republic trying to raise the money to pay reparations from an unwilling citzenry, money-tinkering is always a phenomenon associated with the division of labor—at least until the monetarists actually find some of the "helicopter money" (cash distributed "from thin air" for no particular purpose) that they are always talking about.

Let me explain how those wild blowouts we know as "hyperinflations" fit into this story. To take the most obvious point, I don't mean to say that complexity and prices are somehow magically proportional, that if the CPI goes up 12 percent the world has become 12 percent more complex. The system allows for a lot of play, and a small increase of complexity—the sudden power of OPEC to set prices, for example—can be picked up and amplified many times over, while a greater increase in complexity, such as the advent of paid vacations, may cause barely a ripple. One part of the process of quickly rising prices in the real world resembles nothing so much as a game of "hot potato" in which costs are shifted from actor to actor. This momentum is what economists now call the "core" or "nonaccelerating" rate of "inflation." Complexity enters the picture whenever a new potato is added to the game, with the result that the rate of diffusion speeds up.

Sometimes this "hot potato" game gets out of hand, as in Argentina, where the cost of living now climbs 200 percent per year. Businessmen raise the prices of everything in their stores by 20 percent or so every month, "just like the surfer who has to stay ahead of the waves," as one of them says. It isn't easy to tell someone who lives in Argentina that complexity is at the heart of rising prices, for the complexity of the society doesn't appear to have changed at all; the same Buicks and Oldsmobiles are parked in front of the hotels.

The key to understanding very high rates of "inflation" is usually to be found in the sudden appearance of a major new cost to be borne and in the relative power of the groups it affects to avoid it. In the case of the present rate of inflation in Argentina, it is presumably the anticipated cost of the Falkland Islands war that dramatically kicked up the rate of the price increase. A look back at the annual rate of inflation in Argentina, however, turns up a history of spiking inflation rates with no corresponding external wars to explain them; instead, there is an internal cycle of attempts by businessmen or unions to "break out" of the pass-along chain, followed by crackdowns and controls. This process has been described convincingly by the English economists Dudley Jackson, H. A. Turner, and Frank Wilkinson as "strato-inflation." They write that "the upper and lower boundaries of strato-inflation are determined largely by psychosocial relations to, and a consequent feedback effect on, the going rate of general price increase."

It is here, I think, that the complexity hypothesis fits what Mancur Olson has to say. Olson, a brilliant economic theorist, attracted a great deal of attention two years ago with his book *The Rise and Decline of Nations,* in which he offers a crisp and formal way of thinking about how and why people gang up economically on each other in groups. The gist of this hypothesis is that while people in large groups usually fail to act in their collective self-interest (they let George do it, as the saying goes), people in small groups enforce collective actions through such maneuvers as boycotts, unions, and lobbying in order to win special advantages. The result, says Olson, is that stable democratic societies tend to become sclerotic: dense networks of lobbying organizations grow up to stifle the rate of growth.

One of the implications of Olson's theory is that where more or less symmetrical groups of workers—whom he calls "distributional coalitions"—have more or less symmetrical power, "inflation" is the likely outcome as each group tries to avoid paying whatever costs on the economy are imposed from outside. In the case of oil, the reaction of the distributional coalitions of the West to the sharp ecalation of costs at the hands of OPEC was relatively mild: there was no widespread sense of powerlessness, and the central bankers of the world were able to hold on; in the case of the reparations demands made on the people of Germany after World War I, however, the coalitions of businessmen and laborers were utterly intransigent; the central bank had very little choice but to go on endlessly "validating" the spiral, and in the end, it got completely out of hand. The Weimar Republic coupled indignations with expectations. The result was the death of the German mark.

Yet in the case of Weimar as in the case of OPEC, the crucial thing to look for is the *new* cost that has been added to the equation. It is the underlying complexity of the situation that has changed or is about to change. Simple attention to the money supply is not enough.

SOME QUALIFICATIONS

Thus I do not mean to say that complexity is the only systematic factor that affects price levels. Supply and demand also play their roles, just as they always have. A large part of this book is devoted to sorting out the differences between these two explanatory principles, the two lenses of complexity and equilibrium. Likewise, the rate of increase in the money supply—the accommodation rate—is certainly a factor in the rate of price increase; it is just that thinking about the money supply doesn't offer a very good framework for thinking about the price level. Yet even with this, complexity doesn't explain everything.

Nor do I wish to give the impression that price levels are the only reason for studying the idea of economic complexity. It is only that they are just the most pressing problem in which it is implicated. There are many other thorny problems in which this new idea of complexity will come in handy, from considering the fragility of the economy to the design of work to the balance of payments. However, these topics are not under consideration here.

Neither does the complexity hypothesis entail a proposition about why complexity increases: there are many fine books about that. Ester Boserup thinks that population pressure drives the diffusion of technology. Douglass North says that an analysis of transaction costs can explain the rise of the modern state. Certainly the maximizing behavior of individuals has much to do with the growth of economic complexity, but I think that there will also turn out to be other reasons for this growth. For example, William H. McNeill has argued for the centrality of war and disease as engines of technical change.

Finally, I certainly do not argue that the conduct of monetary policy "doesn't matter." What the Federal Reserve System does obviously matters very much; good technique and sound objectives are of the highest importance in managing the financial system. Even so, I think, it is the changing complexity of the division of labor that ultimately drives the cost of living, not control of the money supply. It may turn out that Paul Volcker is more like Canute with good timing than Horatius at the bridge—although in the short run surely it isn't helpful for us to think so.

COMPLEXITY AND GEOGRAPHY

Now we seem to have completed the trick of fashioning a dynamic vocabulary for discussing complexity, prices, and money —one that will deal with the Darrow model and with the rough outlines of price history. Ironically, however, it is an entirely static comparison that provides one of the most telling reasons for preferring the complexity hypothesis to the Quantity Theory. Economic complexity is particularly useful when considering the factors that cause the purchasing power of money to vary from one place to another.

It is well known that the dollar goes further in the country than in the city, further in the Sunbelt than in the Frostbelt. And why not? Prices are higher in the Northeast than in the Southwest. Every year or so I write a story based on one indicator or another of the cost of living—usually one compiled by a consulting firm that specializes in making cost-of-living adjustments for large corporations. These stories are always widely read.

For example, one very careful study in 1982 found that the cost of a pleasant standard of living—a house in the suburbs, two cars, dinner in a restaurant a few times a year—varied greatly depending on where you lived. In New York, it took $46,500 to buy the bundle. In Minneapolis it was $41,800. In Raleigh, you could do it on $37,100, while in Phoenix, $35,200 was enough. The cost of a *very* pleasant standard of living, whose benchmark was a salary of $80,000 a year, differed even more, also depending on where it was bought. In other words, the purchasing power of money could be 25 percent greater or 33 percent less, depending on where and how it was spent.

I can't prove it, but I have a hunch that much of the reason for this geographic variation has to do with economic complexity. Of course population density—the demand for a limited supply of land as reflected in what economists call the "rent gradient"—plays a major part in establishing the variation, probably the lion's share. But of the rest, I think it is probable that the sheer number of different kinds of jobs and their dense interrelationship in the cities is what makes for the 65-cent cup of coffee in New York City versus the 50-cent cup of coffee elsewhere. After all, it costs $7 million a year alone just to clean the Sunday *New York Times* from the streets of the Big Apple. Those costs must be paid ultimately by consumers in the form of higher prices.

Once again, the point is that it isn't differences in the quantity of money that lead to these differences in its purchasing power. The population is greater in cities than in towns because cities are where the jobs are—in other words, complexity largely explains density. There is more money in city banks than in country banks for the same reason. As ever, complexity and money go hand in hand: travel the Canadian border, if you doubt it, to see the difference between the sort of development fostered by accommodating money (on the American side) and tight money (on the Canadian side).

But once again, the cognitive issue is the controlling one: when you take $50 to Iowa City, it goes further than it would in Manhattan, not because it is a greater sum relative to the rest of the money in town, but because it is buying a somewhat less complex bundle of goods and services.

5

THE COMPLEXITY HYPOTHESIS II

WE MAY NOW RETURN TO THE NUMBERS THAT WERE INTRO-
duced at the beginning of the last chapter. The great virtue of
the English monetary record is that it is continuous; contracts
have been written in pounds, shillings and pence for a thousand
years.

Between the thirteenth century, when the Phelps Brown data
started, and the middle of the twentieth century, when they left
off, there were two sustained and unreversed "price explosions." There appears to have been a third explosion that ended
just as the data began; there appears to be a fourth texplosion in
our times whose end is not yet in sight. To put it another way,
the purchasing power of the British penny over a basket of
food, cloth, and fuel suffered not one but four dramatic dimi-
nutions. Is there any reason to think that economic complexity,
prices, and money are systematically related in the larger world
that is southern England? It seems to me that the answer is yes.

It is remarkable how our understanding of the timing of the
major economic revolutions in Western Europe and England
corresponds to the shape of the Phelps Brown numbers. The
evidence is quite rough, of course, but those times that econom-

ic historians have been inclined to describe as periods of stability, crisis, or contraction have been eras of stable or falling prices, while those periods they have described as expansionary, revolutionary, or as takeoffs have coincided with steadily rising prices that climbed to new levels and then stayed there.

THE STEPWISE PATTERN

Let us recall the numbers. In English price history, there are two, but only two, long intervals, each of about a hundred and thirty years, of genuine price stability: 1380-1510 and 1630-1750. The first stable period ran roughly from the days of Chaucer through Agincourt and the Wars of the Roses to the accession of Henry VIII in 1509. The second period ran from the eve of the English Civil War to the dawn of the Enlightenment—the years of the Ancien Régime, the age of Newton. In each of these long periods of calm, the price level twitched up or down, often with nothing more than the harvest. But always it returned to its prior level.

Then there are two periods when the price level slips downward slightly—"secondary secular movements," as they are called, or ages of mild "deflation" we might say: 1270–1380 and 1815–1899. The first of these is the period of the Black Death, of Wat Tyler's rebellion—the century described by Barbara Tuchman in *A Distant Mirror*. The second runs from the Congress of Vienna to the beginning of the Boer War.

Yet the most striking aspects of this "inflation history" are the three long periods when the price level rose, year after year, for decades at a time, before stabilizing on a previously unprecedented plateau.

The first price explosion occurred during the period 1180-1215, or the twelfth-century renaissance, as it is called, when London Bridge was built and the cathedral at Chartres begun, the university at Oxford founded, the Third and Fourth Crusades mounted, and the Magna Carta signed. The timing was anything but precise, but throughout the twelfth century prices tended to go up. Robert Lopez simply says that between 1150 and 1325, the cost of living quadrupled.

The second price explosion lasted from 1510 to 1630, or roughly from the time Columbus completed his reconnaissance of the New World to the successful settlement of the Massachusetts Bay Colony. Throughout the reigns of Henry VIII, Elizabeth I, and James I, the cost of living in southern England rose persistently, year after year, never very rapidly by modern standards but enough that the commoners were widely aware of the phenomenon. When Shakespeare died in 1616, the price level in London stood perhaps four times higher than when he was born in 1564.

The third of these explosions, from 1750 to 1815, was not as steep. It was caught up with, and perhaps camouflaged by, the Napoleonic Wars and the American and French revolutions and was almost simultaneous with the sixty-year reign of George III. When this episode ended, the price level, as measured by the Phelps Brown index, stood twice as high as it had been seventy-five years earlier.

The fourth episode of rising prices, which to all intents and purposes began in the 1890s, is still unfolding today.

THE STRUCTURE OF ECONOMIC REVOLUTIONS

I should acknowledge that this manner of looking at the long-term history of England is quite different from the usual one. We all but ignore the local controversies originated by professional economic historians: even W. W. Rostow's stage theory is neglected, despite its concept of intricately intertwined commercial, agricultural, and transportation revolutions in the two hundred years before the industrial "takeoff." Rostow's fascinating thesis is unflinchingly "economic" in its viewpoint; where we see complexity, he sees relative price shifts. On the other hand, to political historians, it is the seventeenth century and not the sixteenth that is the century of revolution.

Yet these price data give us a terrific focus for talking about history. They permit us to ask with great forthrightness what these periods had in common. Perhaps the first person to identify the stepwise pattern that shows up so clearly in the Phelps Brown index was François Simiand, a French economist (and a close collaborator of Émile Durkheim) who sought in 1932 to account for the Great Depression by looking backward. Sifting through the data, he distinguished four periods (1500–1650, 1789–1815, 1850–1880, and 1900–1920) of economic expansion—of rising prices and increasing production—that he labeled "A phases." They were interrupted by what he called "B phases," in which production contracted and prices were stable or falling. These were the "secular trends" of prices and production, Simiand said; they included all the other little variations as the tide contains the waves. The pattern he found corresponds very nicely to what the Phelps Brown data have to tell.

Historians have long recognized the twelfth, sixteenth, and eighteenth centuries as periods of economic revolution. Not that there is any unanimity as to which was the crucial juncture at which the "rise of the West" began. To David S. Landes, for example, all commercial and industrial change before the eighteenth century was "essentially superficial." To W. W. Rostow, we must go to the sixteenth century to discover "how it all began." But to R. Allen Brown, "God only knows by what double twist of mental aberration the sixteenth century of the English Tudors and Imperial Spain is somehow 'modern' and thus more 'relevant' than the twelfth of Norman and Angevin, Capetian and Hohenstaufen." At least historians agree that these revolutions are pan-European; though there are differences in their timing from north to south and east to west, they were a shared experience from the twelfth century on.

Can it be stipulated that these revolutions were marked by dramatic increases in the extent of the division of labor? Frankly, beyond a few impressions, it is hard to tell. Nothing resembling "data" is available about the changing division of labor. Yet a look at the history books suggests that specialization has indeed proceeded, coincidentally with rising prices, roughly along the lines that the complexity hypothesis would lead us to expect. Cities, of course, are a great leading indicator of complexity, and so is money, for obvious reasons.

What I propose is that we try to see these revolutions as phases of breakthrough (rather than "takeoff") followed by periods of "mopping up." The breakthrough phase corresponds to periods of rising prices; the "mopping up" periods correspond to stable or even falling prices. Elsewhere, I have suggested a distinction between Type A and Type B complexity, between making new and different and often more expensive things and making the same old things more cheaply. The periods of price explosion involve the "birth" of sectors—new industries, new classes, new types of work, and new products—of changes in the way men think of themselves. So in the twelfth century we find a "new kind of man," says George Duby. In the sixteenth century, Tawney locates "the rise of the gentry." The finance capitalist is a creature of the eighteenth century, according to Eric Hobsbawm, and so on; the list of newcomers is long.

Not that there was an absence of change in the English economy during those long periods of relative calm in the price level. On the contrary, the fifteenth, seventeenth, and nineteenth centuries were times of relative order, each displaying increasing efficiencies and economies of scale. There was something deserving to be called an agricultural revolution in the first of these centuries; a commercial revolution in the second; a transportation revolution in the third. But these involved no very radical departure from the trail that had been blazed in the previous period. Each involved a carrying through rather than a breaking out.

Keep in mind that by inquiring after the rhythms of economic development—of burgeoning complexity—we are intruding into one of the most sophisticated and vital debates in all of economic history. The literature on Rostow's thesis alone fills a five-foot-long bookshelf. Moreover, we will entirely leave out of our considerations the topic of population and the economic effects and causes of its increase on the grounds that the relationship among three variables—complexity, prices, and money—is quite enough for one book. But I think even a quick look at this indescribably rich tapestry is justified, because it is one more way to drive home the possibility that overall economic complexity is directly related to the cost of living. To some, the very mention of the terms "division of labor" and "inflation" in the same sentence is anathema. But to be confronted with the overall history of each, even in the sketchiest form, surely makes one wonder: for nearly a thousand years, when specialization has increased, so has the cost of living, sometimes rapidly, sometimes slowly.

A SHORT HISTORY OF SPECIALIZATION

The England that William I conquered in 1066 was like the Normandy from which he had come: a collection of small villages separated by great forests and a few rudimentary cities hardly bigger than towns, perhaps built within the ruined bulwarks of the Roman cities. A manor house, a church, and a few long peasant huts clustered around, with presses, mills, and barns behind, were the basic communities in which life was organized. There was a state of sorts, with courts, sheriffs, and mints, but in general, men in eleventh-century England scratched in the earth for a living. In the century after the Conquest, only a slow building up of the economic infrastructure took place. Feudal customs were installed, and the water mill, the heavy plow, the three-field system of crop rotation, the horseshoe, and horse collar spread gradually through the kingdom.

Then, however, a series of real changes took hold, first demographic and agricultural, then in the industrial and service sectors. The wave of specialization seems to have come around the end of the eleventh century, at just about the time of what William Beveridge calls "the price explosion of the Middle

Ages." Thus Carlo M. Cippola calls the twelfth and thirteenth centuries the period of "the great expansion"; Robert Lopez calls it "the Commercial Revolution" and says that "here for the first time in history, an underdeveloped society succeeded in developing itself, mostly by its own efforts"; and Douglass North and Robert Paul Thomas state that "economic specialization came into its own." International trade blossomed; annual fairs were set up. The "construction sector" came to have meaning as many cathedrals began to be built. The cloth trade emerged as a major industry; commercial traders emerged as a class. The compass, the vertical loom, and especially the contract were invented. There were no very precise boundaries to the revolution; it was centered in northern Italy, and it continued well into the thirteenth century. Contemporaries of Dante had the sensation of living amid great technical change, according to Carlo Cippola. In England, London's population grew to around 40,000 during the thirteenth century (Florence's was perhaps 200,000), and 2,200 charters for English fairs and markets were given out between 1200 and 1275. Between 1086 and 1346, the population of England grew from perhaps 1.1 million to 3.7 million. Historians agree that around 1300, however, the revolutionary impulse petered out. Why? Douglass North and Robert Paul Thomas, ever alert to the economic interpretation, argue that property rights were insufficiently enforced. There is no agreement about this stall, but things settled into a new routine—and the same can be said for prices.

The fourteenth and fifteenth centuries also have a coherence apart from the Phelps Brown numbers. This was the period whose passage on the Continent was characterized by Johan Huizinga as "the waning of the Middle Ages." Aside from the elegiac quality Huizinga found in its songs and poetry, it is hard to say much good about it. It was a period of war and plague; of the eighty million persons thought to have been alive in Europe in 1347, twenty-five million died in the next two years. Cippola says that the age of the *Cantico delle Creature* gave way to the age of the *Danse Macabre*. When men recovered from the horror of the Plague, they started fighting—and kept on doing so. The Hundred Years' War in France ended just about the time that the thirty-year-long Wars of the Roses began in England (1455-85). Yet the Plague also saw the beginning of what Thorold Rogers later describes as "the Golden Age of English Labor." Suddenly there was a surplus of land to be farmed; bread cost less, and thanks to the labor shortage, wages were rising. There was no great discontinuity in these two centuries: the manorial system survived throughout. If you look at the paintings of Pieter Brueghel the Elder, you get a vivid picture of what life must have been like in the fourteenth and fifteenth centuries. But of course by Brueghel's time—from about 1525 to 1569—the economic world had begun another period of deep change. Again, "the" revolution (it was actually many revolutions) took the form of increasing specialization. Beginning in about 1520, it was to last for perhaps a hundred and twenty years.

As there had been in the twelfth century, there was again a terrific opening up of the physical world, this time in the form of the voyages to the New World. Rostow calls this period "the commercial revolution" and dates it from Bartholomew Diaz's rounding the Horn of Africa in 1488. It was also the period in which Karl Marx located the rise of the bourgeoisie ("the Rosy Dawn" of capitalism, he called it) and the time of the Reformation, whose economic effects have excited much attention because of Max Weber's thesis implicating the Protestant ethic in the spread of capitalism in sixteenth-century England. The scientific revolution is held to have begun in 1600, with the age of Bacon, Galileo, and Descartes. G. R. Elton has described a revolution in government finance as household methods gave way to bureaucracy, writing that "the plain fact is that Henry VII ascended to the throne of a medievally governed kingdom, while Elizabeth handed to her successors a country administered on modern lines."

Thus, talk of the emergence of the modern nation-state goes well below the surface of political theory to the division of labor itself. The sixteenth century also saw what John Nef has called "the First Industrial Revolution," owing partly to the New World and East Indies voyages, partly to the stimulus of an energy crisis in which wood was largely replaced by coal as fuel. Whole new industries evolved: tobacco, silk, lead mining, glassblowing, and printing. Styles of organization and finance also changed dramatically: there was a new sort of merchant, more like a soldier, described by Lucien Febvre as "a man of swift decision, of unusual physical and moral energy, of an unrivalled boldness and determination." As usual, the cities were the leading indicators of economic complexity: Karl Helleiner speaks of the "mushroom growth, in the century from 1550 to 1650, of large and very large urban centers." Is it accidental that this was a period of continually rising prices?

Yet once again the history books tell us that things settled down—there is no generally agreed-upon reason for it. Prices stopped rising. England stopped changing in the deep ways it had for a century and settled into a new routine. By the time the Civil War began in 1642, prices had leveled off from their century-long climb, and they stayed more or less on their new plateau throughout the war. As Phelps Brown puts it, presenting his data, "For a century or more, it seems, prices will obey one all-powerful law; it changes and a new law prevails; a war that would have cast the trend up to new heights in one dispensation is powerless to deflect it in another."

There is again a nice integrity to the period. The seventeenth century is variously dubbed "the Age of Mercantilism" (i.e., of the commercial wars) or of "England's apprenticeship." Sir George Clark writes that "the long economic process of the price revolution, through which the wealth of Europe had expanded, came to an end, to be followed by a new phase of restriction and new commercial conflicts between states. After two centuries of advance there was a pause in geographical discovery and in colonization." From the Restoration of Charles II in 1660 until William Pitt's ministry in 1756 amid the war against the Austrians, Russians, and French, it was an era of familiar enemies, slowly spreading Whig influence, and stable money. Financial events seemed to loom large: as Master of the Mint of England, Newton himself fixed the value of the pound in 1694 amid the first great debates about monetary theory, and the South Sea Bubble of 1720 excited attention around the world. Yet the price level scarcely fluttered on its plateau.

For the first time, we find contemporary accounts of forces other than money shaping the cost of living: John Cary, a Bristol merchant, writes in 1695 that "the refiners of sugar lately sold for sixpence per pound what yielded twenty years since twelvepence; the distillers sell their spirits for one third part of what they formerly did; glass bottles, silk stocks and other manufactures (too many to be enumerated) are sold for half the prices they were a few years since, without falling [i.e., lowering the wages of] the labor of the poor." The reasons he offered for stable prices mostly had to do with Type A complexity.

It proceeds from the ingenuity of the manufacturer and the improvements he makes in his ways of working: thus the refiner of sugars goes through that operation in a month, which our forefathers required four months to effect; thus the distillers draw more spirits and in less time . . . than those formerly did who taught them the art. The glass maker hath found a quicker way of making it out of things which cost him little or nothing. Silk stockings are wove instead of knit. Tobacco is cut by engines instead of knives. Books are printed instead of written. Deal boards are sawn with a mill instead of men's labor. Lead is smelted by wind furnaces instead of blowing with bellows; all of which save the labor of many hands so the wages of those employed need not be lessened.

So specialization was increasing through this period of stable prices, but in a way that was entirely consistent with what we would expect. The seventeenth century is sometimes accused of harboring a "commercial revolution" of its own, and, indeed, the differentation of merchants that occurred was important: "value added" merchants, concerned with standardization and quality control, joined the familiar "gains from trade" sorts who were little more than arbitrageurs and adventurers. (Charles Kindleberger finds the dictum "commerce leads to industry" too simple.) But the basic fact is that the London of Samuel Pepys looked for the most part like the London of Samuel Johnson—the changes of the years 1660–1750, though profound, were gentle affairs compared with those that came before and after.

That events of the eighteenth century changed the human landscape is a truism. People may differ slightly over exactly how to date the Industrial Revolution, but they don't dispute its existence. In 1750 the world still had an agricultural appearance; by 1804 Blake was writing about "dark Satanic mills." What precisely happened? David S. Landes, the author of the finest book on the change, put it this way in *Prometheus Unbound:* "In the 18th century, a series of inventions transformed the manufacture of cotton in England and gave rise to a new mode of production—the factory system. During these years, other branches of industry effected comparable advances, and all these together, mutually reinforcing one another, made possible further gains on an ever widening front."

In the Industrial Revolution machines were substituted for humans; engines were introduced, and raw materials became cheap and plentiful. The division of labor that Adam Smith remarked in the pin factory was deep and comprehensive: T. S. Ashton notes that at the beginning of the century, most coal miners were either getters or drawers; by the end, there were holers, hammermen, remblers, punchers, loaders, trammers, hangers-on, and banksmen. The changes in industry were mirrored by changes in agriculture; this was the period of the greatest "enclosures" of common land, familiar to any reader of Marx, who traced their beginnings from the last third of the sixteenth century. Landes estimates that between 1760 and 1815, Britain enclosed millions of acres, allowing far more intensive cultivation of the land—and turning thousands of peasants into refugees. Finally, there was a revolution in mass production and marketing.

What is there in all this specialization to account for rising prices? Landes notes that the sums spent for the little wooden machines were not great: "a forty spindle jenny cost six pounds in 1792; scribbling and carding machines cost a pound for each inch of roller width; a slubbing billy with 30 spindles cost 10 pounds 10 pence." No, the explanation for the rising prices is more likely to be found in external circumstances of war and foreign trading, where the sums were of larger magnitude. For example, Thomas Tooke, a well-known contemporary analyst and collector of prices, ascribed much of the Napoleonic "inflation" to "cost-push" factors such as taxes and shipping losses. Again, we cannot hope to trace the linkages, but we may expect that they existed. As usual, the growth of the different parts of the economy formed a reinforcing whole, a system of greatly expanded world trade. A fascinating question is why, given the extent of the transformation, the price explosion was so mild.

Once again, it is generally agreed that the rate of change moved into a different gear about 1815, although the deeply troubled nature of the times is sometimes glossed over by economic historians anxious to get on with the age of steam. The Napoleonic Wars ended, and prices fell and bonds rose in their aftermath. The Luddites were smashing machines in Nottingham, there were radical riots every year until the massacre at Peterloo in 1819, and then there was talk of revolution—the French kind. Instead, barely perceptibly at first, a new regime took hold. By the time Victoria was crowned in 1837, the sense of promise of this new age was in the air; by the time the last serious talk of political revolt was heard, in 1848, the promise was unmistakable.

The nineteenth century was the quintessential Type B century. It was then that the processes that had been developed during the Industrial Revolution—"front-ended," a businessman might say—were widely applied and began to pay off. Water power, steam railroads, the telegraph, and mass production methods, together with mass merchandising and all of the other paraphernalia of the Industrial Revolution, were spreading across England and throughout the industrializing nations of the world. An unprecedented export boom in cotton and capital took hold, and not just in Britain: world trade doubled between 1800 and 1840, then increased 260 percent between 1850 and 1870. Decreasing returns became increasing returns. Economies of scale that had not existed in the eighteenth century became dominant. In an influential book, *American and British Technology in the Nineteenth Century*, Hrothgar J. Habakkuk compared the appetite of England and America for technology and found that a labor surplus in England held back the rate of diffusion of technical progress. Nevertheless, it was great.

And all this while the price level declined. To quote Landes again:

In the long history of money and prices, from the Middle Ages to the present, there is nothing like it—with the possible exception of milder declines in the decades following the Black Death and in the seventeenth century. Moreover, unlike these earlier periods when falling prices were linked to catastrophe, depopulation and widespread depression, the nineteenth century was a period of peace, of unprecedented increase in numbers and rapid economic expansion. . . . Why, then, this uniquely persistent deflation? The answer lies of course in the uniqueness of the innovations that constituted the Industrial Revolution; never before had there been a cluster of novelties so general in their application and so radical in their implications.

Is it stretching the imagination too much to see in this brief history a pattern that corresponds to the movements of the data, a story of alternating periods of expansion and consolidation, of A phases and B phases, of economic complexity that increases by fits and starts before settling into long, slow periods of smooth increase? I do not think so. There is no doubt that large-scale catastrophe had much to do with earlier periods of stagnant or falling prices. It is true too that the period of sustained progress that began in 1750 has no real parallel in history. Nevertheless, it may be the source of some real increase in understanding to think of economic revolutions as particular kinds of events, not unique in all their features, but substantially the same in their outlines across the ages.

THE DIRECTION OF CAUSATION—YET AGAIN

To be sure, every time there has been a price explosion, there has been an increase in the supply of money big enough to be described as explosive. Usually it has been assigned the blame for rising prices. Indeed, fifty years ago Earl Hamilton, a scholar at the University of Chicago, stirred up a very great controversy when he laid the origins not only of the sixteenth-century price explosion but of the system of capitalist production itself to the influx of precious metals from the New World that took place during that century.

In a celebrated paper entitled "American Treasure and the Rise of Capitalism," published in *Economica* in 1929, Hamilton argues that the New World booty had financed the East India trade, and that it had been plowed into industrialization and had simultaneously caused a great inflation, during which wages lagged behind prices, leading to a great increase in the profitability of business. In a world of thought dominated by such historians of the sixteenth century as Werner Sombart and R. H. Tawney, this was strong medicine; it was a way of turning Max Weber and Karl Marx on their heads. John Maynard Keynes picked up Hamilton's argument and repeated it in the historical volume of his *Treatise on Money*. Keynes writes, "It is the teaching of this Treatise that the wealth of nations is enriched not during Income inflations, but during Profit inflations—at times, that is to say, when prices are running away from costs." Profit inflation was good for you, he said, because it led to industrial growth. Hamilton went on to extend his analysis to the price explosion of the eighteenth century, arguing that profit inflation facilitated the Industrial Revolution during its critical incipient phases. In Hamilton's presidential address to the American Economic Association in 1952, he recommended a worldwide inflation of 1 or 2 percent a year as a means of developing the Third World.

It is certainly true that explosions in the money supply accompany each of our revolutions. Thus, during the commercial revolution of the twelfth century that followed the Dark Ages, coins began to reappear in large numbers; governments frequently debased their value; the velocity of their circulation increased; mining techniques improved. But "the takeoff . . . was fueled not by a massive input of cash but by a closer collaboration of people using credit," says the historian Robert Lopez. "Unstinting credit was the great lubricant of the commercial revolution."

The monetary experience of the sixteenth century is too well known to dwell on. The flow of precious metals into Spain, then to the north of Europe and England; the invention of better mining techniques; the bewildering array of accounting systems and currency issues—all have been exhaustively researched, mainly by students of the Quantity Theory of Money. A fascinating review of the economic literature relating to the price explosion is made by Fernand Braudel and Frank Spooner in the *Cambridge Economic History of Europe*. They ask: "Was money the dependent or the independent variable? This apparently simple question demands several replies. . . . We must remember that everything was inter-dependent; moneys of account, coinage prices, economies, social structures, phases and epochs of history." Money alone wasn't enough to explain what had happened, they conclude.

The period of the Industrial Revolution was also a period of monetary innovation: banknotes began to take over from coins, and country banks expanded all over England and began issuing bearer notes. An elaborate network of lenders and borrowers grew up with the wartime boom. The experience of an exploding money supply and the rising prices it was thought to be causing sparked a controversy over money and credit that hasn't ended yet, but the first phase of the debate started with the publication of Thornton's *Enquiry into the Nature and Effects of the Paper Money of Great Britain* in 1802 and ended with the Bank Charter Act in 1844, which set the framework for modern monetary theory and practice.

But isn't this argument about money and capitalism, or about money and industrialism, simply Martin Feldstein's argument about the senior partnership of money determining the pattern of technical change in health care writ large? Is there any more reason to think that New World treasure "caused" capitalism than that insurance "caused" modern medicine? Isn't it equally plausible that the advent of capitalism "caused" the New World to be found and its treasure looted? The kings and queens who dispatched the voyagers to the New World had highly specific agendas they wanted to finance. There were wars to fight, religious leaders to placate or to be damned, opportunities for investment to be pursued. To argue that the quantity of money was the main force behind the price explosion of the sixteenth century requires an insensitivity to the events that unfolded then, an insensitivity facilitated by the distance in time of the events of that century. But no one who thinks very long about the way in which central banking and modern complexity interact can be comfortable with the generalization that prices rose in the sixteenth century only because an influx of precious metals from the New World led to "too much money chasing too few goods."

If not money, then what is it that causes economic revolutions? What is the mechanism? Why do they occur when they do rather than sooner or later or never? As we have seen, there is plenty of reason to believe that technology and economic organization are closely related and more than a little reason to think that "styles of consciousness" are implicated in the process. But Marxist historiography, at least as it has been

practiced, is too heavy on mechanism and "policy recommen-
dations" and far too light on detail. Marx himself has said that
philosophers for too long had tried to understand the world,
that the time had come to change it. To my mind it is better
that they should resume their efforts to understand it; change
comes easily, from a million other hands.

Without some mechanism to offer, however, complexity is
merely a deus ex machina, hardly better than the Monopoly
game as an explanation of rising prices. In the sixteenth century, the bourgeoisie built houses and hotels and prices went up,
then leveled off when they stopped building; in the eighteenth
century, they started building again and prices climbed again.
What kind of an explanation is that? Why did they build just
then? Why didn't they start earlier? Why did they stop when
they did?

Alas, I don't know. I'm not trying to explain history as much
as to describe it better. What seems likely is that the English
economy did grow in complexity during these periods; prices
increased and the quantity of money grew. These factors are
clearly reciprocally related, and in the most intricate fashion.
Whatever else, the history of rising prices is not "simply" a
matter of too much money chasing too few goods, nor "simply'
a matter of ideas calling forth without difficulty the money necessary to finance them. Far more satisfying than the mechanical
approach of the Quantity Theory is a view that begins with the
history of the division of labor, for as I have said, if you view
the history of prices as simply a matter of the history of money,
you are blind to the history of everything else.

As I mentioned earlier, many scholars in many disciplines
work more or less directly on what might be called "the history
of the division of labor," but it is in the work of the French
historian Fernand Braudel that the concern with the topic is
most manifest. For example, Braudel distinguishes between the
"short duration" of political events and the "long duration" of
institutional time; he dwells on numbers rather than persons;
he is always mindful of the delicate financial relationship be-

tween the public and the private spheres of life. Having written just two books in over fifty years (*The Mediterranean and the Mediterranean World in the Age of Philip II* was published in 1949; *Capitalism and Material Life* was published in two volumes in 1967 and is being reissued in the 1980s as three), Braudel has nevertheless changed the way in which history is practiced. Under his leadership, the Sixth Section of the Ecole Pratique des Hautes Etudes, the center of French historiography, with its journal, *Annales: Economies, Sociétés, Civilisations,* has become an effective alternative tradition to the manner in which economic history is done in the United States, with its emphasis on economic theory. *Annalistes* before and after Braudel—Lucien Febvre, Marc Bloch, Ernest Labrousse, Roy Ladurie, and Philippe Ariès—have created an economic history that is profoundly structural as opposed to "cliometric." But it is Braudel himself who is the exemplar, coming about as close as one can to being an economist while remaining (and this is the all-important distinction) a historian of the division of labor.

Summing up his work on capitalism, Braudel writes: "Every evolved society incorporates several hierarchies, let us call them staircases permitting exit from the ground floor where the mass of the population . . . vegetates; a religious hierarchy, a political hierarchy, and various financial hierarchies. Depending upon the century and the locality, oppositions, compromises and alliances develop among them." This is the picture I want to leave with you at the end of the book—the kernel of a view to rival the economists' picture of a world of "general equilibrium." The complex world is one of connections, chains, textures, fabrics—a realm of ladders rather than a world of "canceling out."

THE "SECOND" INDUSTRIAL REVOLUTION

And what of the sequence of price history that began in the vicinity of 1890? The existence of yet another monetary explosion seems beyond argument. Is there a "modern revolution" to accompany it? Will we look back someday on the years that have passed since the turn of the century and detect changes as deep and profound as those we now attribute to these earlier periods of economic revolution?

Most everyone agrees that something happened around 1890. "A climacteric," it is called in the literature, a change of life. For one thing, real wages began to fall; they had been rising since the Napoleonic Wars ended, but by the end of the century, "the curve was approaching a very definite ceiling," writes Colin Clark. For another, the pace of life speeded up. The years after 1890 saw the beginning of the new technologies of electrical power and motors, internal combustion engines and automobiles, and organic chemistry and synthetics, as well as an integration of mass production and mass distribution that led directly to a revolution in consumer goods. W. Stanley Jevons lived long enough to call it the Second Industrial Revolution, which can be confusing—remember that John U. Nef has discovered a "first" industrial revolution in sixteenth- and early-seventeenth-century England, and Phyllis Deane was characteristically firm that it was in the eighteenth century that the first Industrial Revolution unfolded.

What do we know about this revolution? In England it was a time of great social change. This is the period, after all, whose tensions are familiar to the millions of viewers of *Upstairs, Downstairs* on the Public Broadcasting Service. The Shops Act of 1911, establishing a weekly half-holiday, was heralded as the beginning of the end of Western civilization. Trade unions were growing; new money was everywhere. Picasso, Stravinsky, and even someone who now seems so tame as George Bernard Shaw were leading the way to unprecedented changes in the arts.

The English like to think that World War I was a remarkable turning point in their national life, but long before 1914 there had been signs of a slowdown in British industry. In part, this was nothing more than the catching up of the rest of the world with the England that hitherto had served it as "workshop":

Charles Kindleberger has said, "An exporter with 75 percent of the world market in a commodity, as the British had at various times in cotton textiles, iron rails, galvanized iron, tinplate, locomotives, ships and coal, can have no expectation of maintaining it." It is true that new industries such as the chemical, automobile, and electrical industries arose to take the place of old ones and that the business of building a modern infrastructure kept the English economy surprisingly healthy. But the coal and cotton industries were declining, as were those of steel and shipbuilding; by the time of the Great Depression, English heavy industry was suffering and highly vulnerable; the nation that had led the world in the first Industrial Revolution was flattened by the second.

Thus the value of money remained fairly directly related to what had gone before, especially in England; even though persons who lived in the first two decades of the century experienced it as an era of rising prices, it doesn't seem reasonable to describe it as a price explosion. A pound sterling in 1930 commanded quantities of goods and services that were not substantially different from what it had bought in the past; the Phelps Brown index fluctuated at about 1,200 throughout the 1930s— just about the same value it had in the 1850s, 1860s, and 1870s. To be sure, in the first decade of the century, one heard quite a lot of talk about the soaring cost of living on both sides of the Atlantic. Between 1913 and 1920, wholesale prices nearly tripled in Great Britain and doubled in the United States, but this was related to the war; the cost of living fell again after the war —though not to previous levels.

What then have we got in the forty years from 1890 to 1930? If it was a "second industrial revolution," where was the price explosion? And if it was simply a continuation of the Type A style of the nineteenth century, why did so many people experience it as such a dramatic break with the past? Our closeness to the events of the time must qualify any convincing discussion of these matters. W. Arthur Lewis, the development economist and Nobel laureate, investigated the similarities between the periods 1899-1913 and 1950-79 because they were the only episodes of rising prices in the last century that did not have a major war as a background, he said. He concluded that they had in common only two main factors: there was a real or perceived shortage of primary commodities; and money incomes tended to outrun productivity gains. My hunch is that the period from 1815 to 1939 will eventually come to be seen as one of fundamental unity, and that the dramatic break with the regime governing the division of labor will be seen to have begun, more or less suddenly, in 1939. In any event, to speak of a "price revolution" between 1890 and 1929 is to misuse the term, even if whole small classes were toppled from their security near the pinnacle of English society by changes in the cost of living.

A POST-INDUSTRIAL REVOLUTION?

It was in 1939 that the new dispensation began, at least with respect to prices. A pint of beer was sixpence then; a pack of cigarettes cost a shilling. As early as 1955, the English economist A. J. Brown was calling it "the Great Inflation." (He dated it as having begun in 1939 and ended in 1951.) The rest can be found in yesterday's newspapers. "Inflation" in England, as in the rest of the world, crept in the 1950s, walked in the early 1960s, ran in the late 1960s, and galloped through the 1970s. Mrs. Margaret Thatcher took over in 1979 and applied the monetary brakes; the retail price index, which had peaked at an annual rate of about 20 percent in 1980, has since dropped to an annual increase of around 8 percent. But in 1984 the price level stands at between ten and twenty times what it was in 1939, depending on how it is measured. Today a pint of beer costs eighty pence and a pack of cigarettes more than a pound. It does not look as though prices will return to their 1939 levels anytime soon.

So what are we left with? It seems to me that the changes that began with World War II had government and corporate organization at their heart. In England and in Europe generally, the period was marked by the triumph of the Labour party and by the rise of the "welfare state"; in America, much the same thing took place. The socialization of health care, of unemployment losses, and of a hundred other conditions of life that had formerly gone unrecognized by the law and uncompensated by the state contributed to the rising overhead of the "public household." I should mention that Phelps Brown sees the narrowing of wage differentials between skilled and unskilled laborers as a particularly significant factor in the process of rising prices; it was a "pay explosion," not a price explosion, he has argued. The English economists Dudley Jackson, H. A. Turner and Frank Wilkinson found that wage claims and strike days really soared only as the tax net hit the working poor and began "clawing back" wage gains.

Meanwhile, there was an equally dramatic change in the "private sector" of the world economy. The rise of intricate national and international markets, a communications revolution, and further specialization in a number of new areas, including synthetic fibers and pharmaceuticals, probably increased the pressure on basic prices. The same period saw great changes in corporate management and world capital flows: Alfred Chandler, who describes the invention and the spread of modern managerial techniques in the nineteenth and early twentieth centuries, says, "It is going to be a long time before I write the history of the post-war corporation." And of course the years after World War II were an era of supremely cheap energy.

In sum, a wage-price-tax spiral, much of it technologically driven, was at the root of the rising prices that began in 1939. It would be silly to suggest that the Bank of England and the U.S. Federal Reserve Board had nothing to do with the price rise, but the basic change *causing* "the Great Inflation" was the "mixing" of the mixed economy, not an increase in the supply of money. The dramatic acceleration of "inflation" that took place at the end of the 1960s was the cooking off of processes that had begun long before. If the price explosion of the sixteenth century accompanied the rise of the world capitalist economy, if the price explosion of the eighteenth century accompanied the birth of the industrial economy, then the price explosion of the twentieth century accompanied the creation of the modern mixed economy. Now that the "mixing" is very nearly complete, the price explosion is likely to come to an end. I have summed up the various factors that seem to be at work and set them out in Figure 9.

Certainly this view of the centrality to "inflation" of the cost of government (and of increasingly complex organizations generally), which is intuitive and not supported by a single set of numbers, is in stark contrast to the usual liberal "Keynesian" view of the sources of rising prices. Alan Blinder and Otto Eckstein—two of the very best economic analysts of the sort who are usually inclined to call themselves eclectic—have recently published dissections of the "inflation" of the 1970s, and neither one mentions the cost of government or taxes, much less of health care or spending on defense, as a significant contributor to that "inflation." On the other hand, neither will this view hold much charm for monetarists such as Milton Friedman, Karl Brunner, Alan Meltzer, and William Poole, who think that money creation is the key. It is true that there are some fine economists, such as Walter Eltis in England, John Hotson in Canada, and Assar Lindbeck in Sweden, who assign a central place to taxes in the story of rising prices, but they are a minority. The great majority of professional economists remain skeptical that the growth of modern government had any direct effect on the cost of living.

Yet we must wonder. Have changes in the complexity of economic organization since 1939 really come without any effect on the general price level? Or are the econometric models underspecified? Do they leave out relationships that should be included? In econometrics, eight quarters is a long time; the period before World War II is ancient history. The assumption is that the patterns of the past fifteen or twenty years can be

A SCHEME OF CIRCUMSTANCES THAT ACCOMPANY ECONOMIC REVOLUTIONS

	Commercial Revolution, 1150–1325	Capitalist Revolution, 1520–1640
Price Effects	"Price Revolution of the Middle Ages"	"The Price Revolution"
"Money Supply"	Coins, Contracts, and Credit	New World Treasure, Better Mining Techniques, Sustained Public Credit
Complexity of Economic Organization	Feudal, Manorial Systems, Merchants, Fairs, etc., Rise of Cities	Bourgeoisie, Slavery, Nation-States, Reformation, "Mushroom Growth of Cities"
Population Increase	Sustained Growth Throughout Europe, 1000–1325	Recovery and Rapid Growth, 1500–1600
Physical Integration	Mediterranean Economy	Atlantic Economy
Mentality	Scholasticism	The Protestant Ethic/The Mechanical Philosophy
Ebbing Point	"The Waning of the Middle Ages," "The Calamitous Fourteenth Century"	Mercantilism, Universal Belligerence, Population Recession

Figure 9

projected into the future indefinitely, that we have changed our system nearly all that we are going to, that we know almost everything we need to know. Is this true?

Finally, we may ask whether one of those eras of relative sta-

Industrial Revolution, 1750–1815	Modern Revolution, 1890–1929	Post-Industrial Revolution, 1939–1979?
"The Depreciation of Bank Notes"	"High Cost of Living"	"Inflation"
Paper Money, Country Banks	Central Reserve Banking	Withholding Taxes, Commercial Credit
Factory System, Finance Capitalism, Industrial Metropolis	Mass Production and Distribution, Managerial Capitalism, Vertical Cities	"Welfare State," "Service Economy," Multinational Enterprise, "Megalopolis"
"Vital Revolution"	Steady Growth and Expansion Abroad	Post-War "Baby Boom"
Colonial Economy	World Economy	"Third World," "Gang of Four"
The Enlightenment/ Romanticism	Modernism	Post-Modernism
"High Capitalism," "Imperialism"	The Great Depression	?

bility we have noted—in terms of prices and of the social and economic systems—may be getting under way today. Many people feel that a deep and important change began during the 1970s and that the years from 1979 to 1983 in particular represent a kind of a watershed in the history of the world economy. With computers coming on strong on one side of the equation, with the "tax revolt" and a willingness to tolerate the deleterious effects of tight money apparently being established as continuing facts on the other side (to say nothing, remember, of the economic effects of the dramatic increase in population after World War II), it seems entirely possible that the price explosion is over, at least for the time being. We may have fetched up on the upper shoulder of an S curve. Perhaps a period like that which began in 1840, or in 1660, is what awaits us now, with life settling down for a stable and satisfying run.

WHAT IT TAKES

It will take the work of generations to trace the linkages through which changes in the division of labor and in the money supply acted on each other during a thousand years of English history. To investigate these changes in the manner I suggest, it would be necessary to have a thousand years of something resembling SIC code data for England. Something of a record already exists, at least for the last three centuries: the pioneering economist Geoffrey King started this tradition in 1688, with his *Scheme of the Income and Expense of the Several Families of England Calculated for the Year 1688.* (Among other things, he found that the heads of only 40,000, or 3 percent, of the nation's 1.3 million families worked as tradesmen; England hadn't yet become a nation of shopkeepers.) It would also be necessary to have a history of money at every step of the way in order to examine the issue of interdependence. It would furthermore be necessary to have a methodology for measuring complexity.

Even without (and perhaps especially without) extensive scrutiny, however, one can see the utility of the "way of seeing" to be learned from the game of Monopoly. The British penny, for which a carpenter once worked all day, is now reduced to near worthlessness. The pound, which in the time of Henry

VIII was a fabulous sum to a workingman (a month's wages or more), is now a undistinguished coin that barely buys a pint of beer or a pack of cigarettes. Why? Is this a matter of money alone? Or is it a matter of both economic complexity and money? Is it simply "too much money chasing too few goods"—of paper pounds cheapened by vast abundance? Or is it a matter of change and development, like the Darrow model? Surely enough has been offered here to make one wonder.

6

CONCRETE PICTURES

AT ONE TIME, ECONOMICS WAS FOR GENTLEMEN AND DILET-tantes. Adam Smith was a schoolteacher, David Ricardo a stockbroker, Thomas Malthus a parson, and Karl Marx a journalist. Leon Walras, an inveterate letter writer, was an engineer who managed to lay the foundations of modern macroeconomics with nothing more than brilliant intuition and a heavily thumbed bedside copy of Poinsot's *Elements de Statique*. In their early days, and perhaps even as recently as the 1930s, economic arguments were accessible to any well-educated layman, and the technical opinions of businessmen and bankers were accorded great respect.

Not anymore. As the world has become more complex, so has economics; in two dramatic bursts of self-organization, it went high tech. The first of these occurred during the 1880s, when the American Economic Association was established to weed out the cranks. At first the AEA accepted all comers, and as late as the 1890s its members still seriously considered electing a businessman as its president. Soon thereafter, though, the Ph.D. became a virtual prerequisite for serious work in the field.

Then, at the University of Chicago in the 1940s, the second revolution took place. In the space of a few exciting years, scholars associated with the Cowles Commission learned how to write up the systems of equations of "general equilibrium" of which Walras had dreamed and how to estimate them statistically—that is, they invented econometrics, the marriage of measurement and theory.

The result of this breakthrough was that gentlemanly economic philosophers such as Frank Knight, Joseph Schumpeter, and even John Maynard Keynes were supplanted almost overnight by tough-minded, mathematically oriented kids. To be sure, it was Keynes's ideas about the relationship between employment and the rate of return on investments that were being cranked into these models, but as those who were his interpreters came of age, economics became a field nearly impenetrable to an outsider. When in 1970 Paul Samuelson became the first American to win the newly created Nobel award in economics, he joked that it was odd to find himself in so public a place after having spent his life working on "turnpike theorems and osculating envelopes; nonsubstitutability relations in Minowski-Ricardo-Leontief-Metzler matrices of Mosak-Hicks type; balanced budget multipliers under conditions of balanced uncertainty in locally impacted topological spaces and molar equivalences." Today, the subject has gone far beyond these boundaries to new frontiers.

But underneath, the entire edifice is still built on two relatively simple ideas: the concept of General Equilibrium and the Quantity Theory of Money. These are the subject matter of Economics I. Share these concepts and you are an economist; fail to do so and you are not. They deserve careful examination. An appreciation of their conceptual wellsprings will provide a key of sorts to the question: "Why do technical economists have so little to say about complexity?"

HOW DO SCIENTISTS SEE?

Probably no one person has done as much to transform our understanding of what scientists do and how they do it than Thomas S. Kuhn. Born in 1922, Kuhn is an MIT professor who looks more like a businessman, or even the physicist he was trained to be, than the type of fellow who gets his name carved on the tops of buildings—a modern equivalent of Darwin or Mendeleev. But with the publication in 1962 of a little essay called *The Structure of Scientific Revolutions*, Kuhn set a stamp on the science of the age that may turn out to be as enduring as that of any physical scientist.

Before Kuhn's essay, the dominant conception of science in most quarters was that of a highly rational procedure in which scientists hypothesized about the ways in which things worked, then tried to knock holes in their own and others' arguments— a matter of "conjecture and refutation," in Karl Popper's phrase. Scientists were educated guessers, forever venturing, forever alert to the scrap of fact that wouldn't square, the datum that might falsify their propositions, on the grounds that if this datum didn't prove them wrong, they might be right.

Today, the experts have come to think of science as being somewhat less open to whatever comes along in the investigator's life. According to Kuhn, science is very much a matter of learning to conceive of things in a certain way, to acquire certain habits of thought—so much so, in fact, that even direct experience might be disregarded. "It is the theory which decides what we can observe," Einstein says. Kuhn's book drives the lesson home.

In the early days of the sciences, Kuhn writes, every investigator had to start from scratch until there emerged a shared vision, a plausible idea about the underlying mechanism of a particular phenomenon. This shared understanding Kuhn calls a "paradigm," borrowing the grammatical term for the rules governing the conjugation and declension of verbs and nouns (*"amo, amare, amari..."*).

Once a paradigm is established and has become persuasive to a community of researchers, work can then begin on its further articulation, a process that Kuhn calls "normal science." He compared the enterprise of normal science to "mopping up" after achieving a beachhead in an invasion, or to the efforts of a man who tries to elucidate topographical detail on a map whose outlines are known to him in advance. This "puzzle solving" was what most scientists did most of the time, Kuhn says, and were no less glamorous for it. It simply wasn't "revolutionary." (For many, this stuck in the craw. The idea that paradigms might put some sort of blinders on scientists was repugnant to those who preferred to view science as the one field in which preconceptions played little or no part.)

Every once in a while, however, a paradigm would run into problems it couldn't handle. Unexpected "anomalies" would crop up and vex scientists. Complicated and jury-rigged attempts to explain away the problem would be offered and accepted until a few scientists would suddenly manage to see the problem differently—Kuhn compares the process to a gestalt switch—and the paradigm would begin to shift. The old interpretation would be discarded by most if not all members of the research community, and the new one would become the basis for discussion and further research.

On one point Kuhn is insistent. Only a paradigm can replace a paradigm; you cannot walk away from one interpretation of events without having a better one to put in its place—unless you are willing to abandon the attempt to do science. A scientist who complains about the explanatory power of the view of matters in which he has been trained, without offering an alternative view, is like a carpenter who blames his tools.

Clearly much depends upon the nature of a paradigm. *The Structure of Scientific Revolutions* touched off twenty years of wrangling between historians and philosophers of science over the nature of paradigms. One of the most useful discussions was by Margaret Masterman, a researcher at the Cambridge University Language Unit. She writes that in his book, Kuhn's use of the word "paradigm" could be interpreted in twenty-one distinct senses—as a myth, a textbook, a model, a source of tools, a standard illustration, a gestalt figure, and an organizing principle, among others—a fairly bewildering array of meaning. After a long analysis, Masterman concludes that ultimately, paradigm means a concrete "picture," used analogically, because a paradigm is ultimately a "way of seeing." Masterman says that this crude analogy could be anything—wire and beads made to resemble a DNA molecule, the conceit of man as wolf—but that whatever it was, it would be fundamentally incomparable with any other crude analogy for the same phenomenon.

Here is the exploratory tool that will help us understand the failure of economists to give complexity very much thought. It is all very well to define an economist as someone who sees his field as "the problem of choice" or as someone who sends his papers to the *American Economic Review*. But for the moment, we may inquire if an economist is not one who sees the world as being "like" something in particular in a way that is not comparable with other ways of seeing it. If so, we may wonder what that "way of seeing," what that "concrete picture, used analogically," may be. I propose that we undertake some intellectual archaeology.

WHAT HOLDS IT ALL TOGETHER?

Traditional economics begins in a kind of wonderment, not so much that complexity exists, but that things hang together amid it. "On entering Paris which I had come to visit," writes the French classical economist Frederic Bastiat in the kind of exclamation typical of economists early and late,

I said to myself—Here are a million of human beings who would all die in a short time if provisions of every sort ceased to go towards this great metropolis. Imagination is baffled when it tries to appreciate the vast multiplicity of commodities which must enter tomorrow through the barriers in order to preserve the inhabitants from falling prey to all the convulsions of famine, rebellion and pillage. And yet all sleep at this moment, and their peaceful slumbers are not disturbed for a single instant by the prospect of such a catastrophe. On the other hand, eighty departments have been laboring today, without concert, without any mutual understanding, for the provisioning of Paris.

Why was it that farmers could be counted upon, day after day, to bring their produce to the city? Why did the shopkeepers open their doors? Why would garbagemen always cart the detritus away? Why didn't the whole intricate array of an eighteenth-century economy collapse? There was, after all, nobody directing it.

This was the question implicit in *The Wealth of Nations*. Adam Smith's answer was that a spontaneous order of growing complexity resulted precisely *because* everyone pursued his own self-interest. The economic world was a system connected by a breathtakingly simple mechanism—a system of opposing forces of desire and effort kept in balance by the rational calculation of self-interest by millions of economic actors.

The crucial passage in *The Wealth of Nations* occurs when Smith identifies human self-interest as the motive that accounts for most if not all economic change. He writes:

But it is only for the sake of profit that any man employs his capital in the support of industry; and he will always, therefore, endeavor to invest it in the support of that industry of which the produce is likely to be of the greatest value, or to exchange for the greatest quantity either of money or of other goods. . . . He is in this, as in many other cases, led by an invisible hand to promote an end which was no part of his intention. . . . By pursuing his own interest he frequently promotes that of the society more effectually than when he really intends to promote it.

Kenneth Arrow has put this most basic insight of economics somewhat more technically: there is a tendency toward the equalization of rates of return, enforced by the ability of investors to move from low to higher rates of return, he says. In other words, he says, people will choose what is best for them. The fact that this can be counted on is the beginning of all equilibrium economics.

Out of this axiom slowly grew all the apparatus of modern economics. At first there was simply the idea of negative feedback: when corn prices rose, men planted corn, leading to a greater supply, whereupon corn prices fell back toward their equilibrium price and farmers turned to some other opportunity. Early economics was preoccupied with supply; it took fifty years for it to catch up with demand as a force of equal magnitude. In the early days, economists argued passionately about the price of things such as salt and water. They found it a striking paradox that the most useful things in the world were the cheapest and that the most frivolous items—diamonds and champagne, for example—were the most expensive. The cost of production was for the most part what determined prices, they reasoned; value was something intrinsic to the item in question.

The breakthrough came in three places at once: an Englishman, Stanley Jevons, an Austrian named Karl Menger, and the great French economist Leon Walras. All hit upon the idea, more or less at once, that the value of economic goods was determined subjectively, by their utility to the purchaser, rather than by anything intrinsic in the goods themselves. It had always been clear enough that a rise in price would diminish the demand for corn. The question was why. The answer supplied by Jevons, Menger, and Walras was that corn purchasers were always sizing up the extra satisfaction that would be brought by an extra pound of corn at such and such a price as compared with all the other available goods and services. Out popped the idea of marginal utility. Workers didn't spend all their money on beer; they made choices. "Economic man" was someone who maximized his marginal utility through substitution: each cup of sugar, each bottle of beer, was demanded precisely up to the point at which its marginal utility was equal to the marginal utility of a dollar spent on any other good.

The nature of Adam Smith's "invisible hand" was becoming clearer. It was Walras who saw that because of this principle of substitution at the margin, the relations between all the quantities supplied and all the prices asked of all the commodities offered for sale in the world could be expressed in a gigantic series of simultaneous equations in which everything depended on everything else—in which the quantity of a good demanded was a function not of its price alone but of the entire constellation of prices. It earned him the admiration of the historian Joseph Schumpeter, who called him the author of economics' "Magna Carta." Some seventy-five years later, a group of economists and statisticians working in Chicago figured out how to implement Walras's grand vision, how statistically to estimate the equations that represented the countervailing power of the modern economy, its savings flows and consumption patterns. With this, modern econometrics was born. Today, thanks to this notion of general equilibrium, economists can frame a precise answer to virtually any economic question, from the most general to the most precise. What, for example, will happen to coffee prices in Milan if there is a bad tea harvest in Ceylon? But all this is described in an elementary economics text; the point here is to inquire after the idea that is concealed in "the invisible hand."

THE IDEA OF GENERAL EQUILIBRIUM

Does General Equilibrium theory constitute a paradigm? Is there a "concrete picture, used analogically" at the bottom of it, as Margaret Masterman might expect? Yes, but it doesn't have anything to do with a hand, invisible or otherwise. I believe that instead, the idea of an ordered system whose complexity is unimportant because everything depends on everything else—a system held together by negative feedback, in other words—is the same concept that Copernicus, Kepler, Galileo, and finally Isaac Newton discerned in celestial equilibrium and then described over a period of one hundred and fifty years in the sixteenth and seventeenth centuries; in fact, I believe that there is a fairly direct correspondence between the picture of the economic world arranged by the canceling out of opposing forces in balance, as it has been interpeted by economists down through the years, and the gravity-ruled physical universe that Newton discovered. Economists believe that the invisible hand of universal competition holds the economic world together and regulates behavior in it just as the law of gravity holds the physical universe together.

Even today there is some disagreement about exactly what Newton accomplished when he published his *Principia* in 1686. Newton himself says that he was out to explain "the motions of the planets, the comets, the moon and the sea." On the surface, it was as simple and astonishing as that. The theory of universal gravity, with its sweeping organization of the study of motion through the concepts of mass, force, and acceleration, has provided a key to understanding everything that moves. It may be, as I. Bernard Cohen has argued, that there was something even more than this to the Newtonian revolution—that the philosopher invented the very *style* of combining mathematical modeling with experimental method that we consider as being "scientific." But for those eighteenth-century scientists who basked in the glow of the Newtonian discoveries, it was enough to know that Newton had discerned the mechanism of the "invisible hand" that held the physical universe together.

Certainly economists have often enough explained their insights into the workings of the economy in Newtonian terms. The analogy runs through two centuries. Adam Smith lectured on astronomy, and while he stopped short of comparing himself to Newton, his pride clearly ran deep for having uncovered the "connecting principle" of economic affairs—that prices are continually "gravitating" to their natural level. Alfred Marshall, reviewing Stanley Jevons's work in 1872, puts the vision of general economic equilibrium this way: "Just as the motion of every body in the solar system affects and is affected by the motion of every other, so it is with the elements of the problem of political economy." Reviewing Marshall's career fifty years later, John Maynard Keynes writes of how "the proposition that value is determined at the equilibrium point of demand and supply was extended so as to discover a whole Copernican system, by which all the elements of the economic universe are kept in their places by mutual counterpoise and interaction."

It is true that there are many different paths to the idea of equilibrium, including the route from ecology, which is apparently the one that French economists such as Turgot and Quesnay followed, but the main road to the modern conception was the idea of mechanical equilibrium, and as the understanding of mechanics was continually refined in the physical sciences during the nineteenth century, so was the notion of equilibrium pursued in economics. Jevons writes in the preface to his *Theory of Political Economy* that in its new marginalist incarnation, economics "presents a close analogy to the science of Statical Mechanics, and the Laws of exchange are found to be the Laws of equilibrium of a lever as determined by the principle of virtual velocities. The nature of wealth and Value is explained by the consideration of indefinitely small amounts of pleasure and pain, just as the theory of Statics is made to rest upon the equality of indefinitely small amounts of energy." Optimization problems in modern economics are handled by methods devised by LaGrange, the author of the grand synthesis of eighteenth-century mechanics. But if you want to know what is in an econometrician's head when he talks about General Equilibrium, don't worry about the more concrete applications of Newton's laws; think of stars, planets, moons, comets, whirling endlessly in their predetermined paths, in a celestial equilibrium maintained by the "invisible hand" of gravity. Call this vision of economists the "general balance theory" of the economic world.

Here, then, is some illumination of why an economist doesn't see complexity when he examines systems that are worth thinking about. After all, the degree of complexity of a system in equilibrium is quite beside the point, which is the overall balance of the countervailing elements. Whether one is dealing with ten stars or ten thousand, the important thing is the interplay of opposing forces, not the number of objects involved; mass and velocity of objects, not types of objects. Similarly, the magnitudes to be measured in order to understand the working of an economic system are elasticities of supply and demand for each individual good, rather than the growing diversity of the goods and the concomitant complexity of the system. Oscar Morgenstern comes close to acknowledging this distinction when he suggests that economists had a harder time of it than astronomers because "we know that our economies are subject to tremendous and rapid changes, while up to [the time of] Newton and for Newton's purposes the sky could be considered static," referring to the seemingly unchanging complexity of the heavens.

The "general balance" approach is obviously a highly useful way of thinking about economics; but it is not the only way. It is a different approach from one that has complexity at its heart. The two aspects of an economic system, its complexity and its internal cohesion, are irreconcilable; you can't see the same system in both philosophical lenses at the same time. When considering complexity, the familiar lingo of General Equilibrium analysis—of supply side and demand side—has little meaning. What is of interest is the degree of connectivity of economic agents, of interface, of diversity, and not the tension between buyers and sellers. In the analysis of complexity, the essential features are additive; with equilibrium, things always "net out."

Recognizing that this General Equilibrium analysis is the basis of economics gives the outsider a leg up in understanding what the community of economists is doing. Like mapmakers who know in advance the outlines of a terrain, economists are busy extending the equilibrium analogy to everything under the sun. New labor economics? New industrial organization? These are merely new ways of extending the analysis of supply and demand to new fields, such as the supply and demand for information. Economists speak of a deepening of their understanding of events, not of a change of understanding. This beautiful idea of the counterbalancing forces of incentive and desire remains the core of economic thought.

The General Equilibrium is by no means the entire story of economics, however. The other concept that all economists hold in common is, of course, the Quantity Theory of Money.

THE QUANTITY THEORY OF MONEY

The Quantity Theory also has a long and distinguished pedigree. From Copernicus, who wrote a book about prices in Poland in the sixteenth century, through John Locke and Isaac Newton in the seventeenth century, to David Hume and Adam Smith in the eighteenth, W. S. Jevons and Simon Newcomb in the nineteenth, and Irving Fisher, John Maynard Keynes, and Milton Friedman in the twentieth century, the Quantity Theory has been passed from one generation to another, with each adding something of its own. Today, the theory is widely shared and highly developed, and yet it is capable of as simple an expression as David Hume gave it more than two hundred years ago in writing that "it seems a maxim almost self-evident, that the prices of every thing depend upon the proportion between commodities and money, and that any considerable alteration on either has the same effect, either of heightening or lowering the price. Increase the commodities, they become cheaper; increase the money, they rise in their value [price]."

First, notice that there is nothing here of negative feedback, of the idea of supply and demand. Instead of "balance," the key idea seems to be one of "proportion," and inverse proportion at that. There is nothing self-equilibrating about the money supply, at least as the Quantity Theory explains it. It is a wonderfully simple idea: to keep prices low and the purchasing power of money correspondingly high, keep money tight, or at least growing at a predictable rate, year after year.

Over the centuries there have been many disagreements about exactly what money is. Is it gold? Gold and silver? Paper money? What about credit? Money is usually defined as "anything that is acceptable for payment in ordinary transactions," but where do you draw the line? How do you tell the difference between the kind of money that people use for spending—whose quantity has a direct link to prices—and the kind they use for saving, whose quantity is much more loosely regulated? Since money-creating institutions like banks are constantly changing the kinds of services they offer, these controversies have been going on for centuries. In fact, because banks learned to create it so well, through the practice of fractional lending against their reserves, economists developed an entire series of measures of different kinds of money, having periodically drastically revised their definitions of money to take account of the changing nature of the banking system. Such a change is going on now, as deregulation of the American banking system makes for pronounced changes in the liquidity (the spendability) of certain forms of money.

Likewise, there has been a lively and continuing development in yardsticks designed to measure the "inflation of prices" that increasing money is believed to cause. The price index was invented by William Fleetwood, bishop of Ely, in response to a question from an Oxford undergraduate wondering whether to accept a scholarship. Was the money it entailed worth as much as it used to be? Fleetwood's answer was to compile a market basket to serve as a crude guide to the purchasing power of money. "Since money is of no other use, than as it is the thing with which we purchase the necessaries and conveniences of life," Fleetwood writes, "'tis evident that if five pounds in H. VI days would purchase 5 quarters of Wheat, 4 Hogsheads of Beer and 6 Yards of Cloth, he who then had 5 pounds in his pocket was full as rich a man as he who now has 20 pounds, if with that 20 pounds he can purchase no more Wheat, Beer and Cloth than the other."

But suppose the price of beer goes up and wheat comes down. Won't the student drink less and eat more? And won't all prices change in response? And suppose the cloth is cotton one year and nylon the next? How then do you measure inflation? And what exactly does "full as rich" mean? These are some of the questions that have been raised since Fleetwood wrote, but while there is today in index number theory a great deal of sophistication about substitution and technical change, the modern CPI is a direct descendant of Fleetwood's basket, and the idea is still much the same.

Economists like to write up relationships such as this one between money and prices in the form of mathematical equations, in order to clarify them, and there are many different ways to describe the relationship between money and prices. The best-known equation is $MV = PT$, where M is the supply of money; V is its velocity or the number of times it changes hands within some time period; P is the price level, or the average price of each transaction; and T the number of transactions. There are various levels of meaning here: at the simplest, the statement equates the value of what is bought to the value of what is sold; expenditures equal receipts. In a restaurant, for example, M might be the average amount of money handed over the counter; V, the number of times that sum is paid; P, the average cost of a meal; and T, the number of meals served. Generalized to the whole economy, M is the quantity of money in existence; V, the number of times each piece of money is used; P, the "general price level," as exemplified by, say, the consumer price level; and T, the aggregate quantity of goods.

Even after Milton Friedman's reformulation of the Quantity Theory as a theory of the "demand for money," in order to square the English approach of zeroing in on the "cash balances" kept on hand by individuals (as an asset, in other words) with the American habit of treating money as a stream, so better to wrestle with the theorizing of John Maynard Keynes, the theory has remained much the same old idea it always was. Despite immense technical subtlety, its essence today remains largely what it was in the time of Hume and Fleetwood. You take a collection of goods and services representative of the regular needs of some wide class of persons, price it, and price it again later. If the price of this market basket has gone up substantially, inflation has occurred; the purchasing power of money has correspondingly shrunk. Inflation means you are paying more for the same market basket, for inflation—as we well know by now—is too much money chasing too few goods.

"TWICE THE MONEY, HALF THE VALUE"

Precisely why do we call it inflation? To this question I think there is really one and only one correct answer. George Shackle, an English economist, hit on it one day in 1955 when he was speaking to a convention of accountants, saying:

How did we come to adopt the portentous word "inflation" to mean no more than a general rise in prices? I think this usage must have had its origin in a particular theory of the mechanism or cause of such a rise. When a given weight of gas is released from a steel cylinder into a large silk envelope, there may appear to be more gas, but in important senses, the amount of gas is unchanged. In a somewhat analogous way, we can make our total stock of currency spread over a larger number of paper notes, but this action in itself will not increase the size of the basket of goods (where various goods are present in fixed proportions) that this total stock of currency would exchange for in the market. . . . Some such image as this may perhaps have been in the mind of the man, who first spoke of inflating the currency. This idea, that the general price level is closely related to the ostensible, apparent size of the money stock . . . has become formally enshrined in what is called the Quantity Theory of Money.

The perceptive reader will recognize as Boyle's Law the metaphor that Shackle used to explain the vocabulary of the Quantity Theory. Though it is no longer an especially significant territory in the geography of the scientific imagination, Boyle's Law, for a century after its formulation in England in 1661, had the same kind of mythic significance for educated persons that Newton's laws enjoyed in the eighteenth century and that Einstein's theories of relativity have in our own time. Thanks to Boyle, we say that twice the pressure on a gas means half the original volume; three times the pressure, one-third the volume; one-third the pressure, three times the volume; and so on. Boyle discovered these precise relationships by pouring increasing weights of mercury into the upper end of a J-shaped tube and by measuring the space occupied by the air in the sealed lower end. This homely mathematical regularity, which sounds so simple today, was one of the first great breakthroughs of the scientific revolution: it was the final elegant demonstration that the atmosphere was, as men had long suspected, "like an ocean of air," its behavior as predictable by men who knew its secrets as that of water.

The parallels between the Quantity Theory and Boyle's Law are striking and direct. While a modern quantity theorist no longer says "double the money, double the prices, half the purchasing power," his recipe is the next best thing. Loose money means high prices and tight money means low prices, just as a large volume means a low pressure and a small volume means a high pressure—for a fixed quantity of gas. Considerable energy has been expended over the years in arguing whether the Quantity Theory entails the idea of a "strict" or "mechanical" proportionality between money and prices, but I think this is a red herring; any two-way relationship between money on the one hand and prices on the other is a form of the Quantity Theory (the inversion of the relationship takes place when the concept of "purchasing power" is employed). In analogic terms, the concrete picture that lurks at the bottom of the Quantity Theory is our understanding of what happens when you blow up a balloon.

Somewhere along the way, probably in England, an understanding of Boyle's Law and precocious insights about money seem to have made a marriage. They grew side by side. William Petty put the idea of velocity into the Quantity Theory in the seventeenth century. The eighteenth century saw work on the "transmission mechanisms" by which increasing money brought about higher prices. By the late nineteenth century, the American astronomer Simon Newcomb had put the Quantity Theory into a formula that soon looked like the notation of Boyle's Law: $PV = K$ for the pressure and volume of a gas versus $MV = PT$ for money and price levels. (Economist Donald McCloskey has noted that the equation is "the same term-for-term as the equation of state of an ideal gas, and has the same status as an irrefutable but useful notion in chemistry as it has in economics.") Irving Fisher, the father of American monetarism, actually described Boyle's Law as an "analogue" in physics to the Quantity Theory. Who should have known better? The relationship between Boyle's Law and the Quantity Theory is clear in the endless pictures of balloons and pumps that decorate tracts on how to fight "inflation" and in the language of analysis itself.*

This concrete picture of a gas and the relationship of its pressure to the volume of its container offers a clue to why economists working from the Quantity Theory find economic complexity so easy to ignore. If the "things of the world" are like a gas, the money supply is like a container, and the price

---

* Nor is monetary economics the only realm of human experience in which the inverse reciprocality of Boyle's Law seems to have explanatory power. There is something similar at work in Parkinson's Law, that work expands to fill the time allowed for its completion.

level is like the pressure, there is no place in the picture for complexity. The relevant fact about the molecules of gas—the "things" of the world offered for sale—is their unchanging homogeneity. A greater "quantity" of them would change only one aspect of the situation—the "pressure," or the price level.

THE MONETARIST AS PLENIST

We have seen how quantity theorists like to talk about "all" prices. From Hume's discussion of the price of "every thing" to Friedman's formulations, there is a curious unwillingness to talk about anything other than the "general" price level, to confront the effect on the price index of changes in complexity of, for example, CAT scanners in medical care. Economists prefer to describe these as "relative price changes" and to say that as long as the money supply doesn't increase, there will be no change in the overall price level. There was nothing intrinsically "inflationary" about OPEC, they say; as long as money stays constant, some prices will go up, other prices will come down. (With OPEC, it was difficult to find prices that came down.) It will all average out. Whence springs this curious reluctance on the part of monetarists to disaggregate their price indexes?

Even when it comes to the game of Monopoly, quantity theorists have a hard time getting "inside" the system, to see how an evolving world might produce rising prices. They say, in effect, "No, no, you've got it all wrong. Inflation means *all* prices are rising—chance cards, land prices, all the rest, must be rising in order to provide an illuminating example of 'inflation.' " I would like to venture why this should be the case.

When an economist speaks of "all" prices or of the price of "every" thing or of "the prices" of things in general, he is making a tacit assumption about the nature of the world—namely, that the inventory of kinds of prices and their relationship to each other doesn't change significantly over time. We have encountered this idea before, as the principle of plenitude. For thousands of years, people conceived of the world as a fixed list of types of things, an order, a "great chain of being" of essentially unchanging complexity. There might be more frogs in one century than the next, but there never would be different categories of things. This sort of worldview facilitated comparison of one period to another.

This peculiar assumption of plenitude is involved in talk of inflation, for it is only when you assume plenitude—that is, assume the absence of technological change—that a comparison between the goods of the world and the molecules of a fixed quantity of gas makes sense. The assumption goes to the root of the idea behind the Quantity Theory: that it was the money that changed and that everything else remained the same. This, I suppose, represents one sense in which the Quantity Theory is valid. If you only could assume plenitude, if the world really didn't change, and if a helicopter did in fact fly over and drop money indiscriminately . . . then the price level probably would rise. But of what use is this insight? The world *does* change, and more often than not the changes affect in some systematic way the prices that we measure and speak of as "the general price level" or "the cost of living." To the quantity theorist, however, this is all ultimately uninteresting. His eyes are on the money supply. Monetarists are plenists, custodians of a faith that passed long ago.

We have begun developing a satisfying answer to the question: "How is it that technical economists have ignored complexity so completely for so long?" The answer has to do with the way in which these economists are organized, not with the way they work (in academic economics departments or in staff offices of big corporations), but instead with the conceptual structure of their intellectual enterprise, the shape of their thinking about the world. In seeing the determination of prices either as a matter of the counterbalance of forces or in terms of the proportion between a particular inventory of things and money, they are a little like the drunk who looks for his lost key beneath the streetlamp "because that's where the light is." And who can blame them?

THE METAPHOR OF THE COMPUTER

Keeping in mind the dictum that "only a candidate can beat another candidate," what metaphor will unlock the secrets of economic complexity? Today there is an influential band of less-than-methodologically-inclined economists who pursue what might be called "the new institutionalism"—they range from policy activists (Barry Bluestone and Bennett Harrison, for example, or Gar Alperovitz and Jeff Faux, or Robert Kuttner) to Marxists (Samuel Bowles, Tom Weisskopf and David Gordon, or Stephen Marglin) to "post-Keynesians" (Edward Nell, Paul Davidson, Robert Heilbroner) to the "evolutionary economists" grouped around the *Journal of Economic Issues*. But these thinkers, provocative as they are, all operate broadly within the conventional framework of economic analysis. Their analyses are often cogent, but they do not constitute a truly different vision of the economic process.

What about some concrete picture drawn from biology? This was Alfred Marshall's great hope, and any number of able economists have echoed him. Yet the answer must be that no such metaphor has yet come to light that is widely consensible. Sometimes a biological analogy can be quite striking: Jane Jacobs occasionally uses them to advantage, as when she asks us to imagine a "goofy arrangement" in which "different individuals [are] hooked up to one brainstem breathing center" in order to imagine the way that national currencies mask feedback information. And there are plenty of people who argue that the economic world is "like" an ecological system and that the relations between competitors resemble biological competition. There even have been a few attempts to rigorously ground the analysis in theory—Kenneth Boulding's *Ecodynamics: A New Theory of Societal Evolution* is the most striking example. But these comparisons lack the power to command widespread assent and professional commitment from experts. The triumphs of the last twenty years in molecular biology notwithstanding, we simply do not understand life processes well enough to draw fruitful comparisons at deep levels between the way living systems operate and the way human communities function.

Every once in a while someone suggests modern thermodynamics as offering a suitable fund of metaphors for an alternative understanding of economics. There is Nicholas Georgescu-Roegen, for example, who in *The Entropy Law and Economic Progress* tries to represent the economic process by a system of equations explicitly modeled on those of thermodynamics. Edward H. (Ned) Allen did something of the same in a dissertation he wrote at the University of Pennsylvania in 1970 ("Complexity and Politicodynamics: A Theory of the Measurement of Development"); so did William Krehm, a remarkable Canadian economic journalist, in his book *Price in a Mixed Economy*. These thinkers approach structures by treating them as "negentropies"; that is, as manifestations of negative entropy. They provide a rough measure of complexity, but not a theory of what creates it. Technical problems aside, however, the trouble with these attempts to draw economic parallels with the tendency of heat or information or anything else to decay is that they often represent nothing more than the observation that in the long run we are all dead. For example, Georgescu-Roegen has written, "The Entropy Law does not help an economist say precisely what will happen tomorrow, next year, or a few years hence. Like the aging of an organism, the working of the Entropy Law through the economic process is relatively slow but it never ceases. So, its effect makes itself visible only by accumulation over long periods. Thousands of years of sheep-grazing elapsed before exhaustion in the steppes of Eurasia led to the Great Migration." It may be a case of the pot calling the kettle black, but I am skeptical of the ability of these views to deliver long-run illumination and guidance in economics. In any event, they are not what I have in mind when I say that what we need is a concrete picture to be used analogically in thinking about complexity.

No, where connectivity, interaction, thresholds, redundancy, differentiation, and hierarchy are the important points, what better metaphor could we hope to discover than that exemplar of the modern age, the computer? The complexity of computers has increased by leaps and bounds in the last fifty years, and so has our ability to talk about them, to measure their capabilities. Indeed, it may be that through the study of "artificial intelligence" we will arrive at a better understanding of life processes, including the mysteries of thought. It would be a wonderful irony if, by lending us the box of conceptual tools involved in its operation and measurement, the computer were to restore to social life some of the coherence that the complexity of the modern world has taken away.

One economist who has done extensive work on the measurement of economic complexity is Peter Albin. Born in 1934, Albin is a an interesting figure in economics. A Yale undergraduate, he was trained in economics at Princeton; Burton Malkiel, one of his teachers there, remembers that "he was a little exotic even then."

Albin drifted away from equilibrium economics during a sabbatical year at Cambridge in 1970, when he first encountered the game of Life, a pastime devised by John Horton Conway, a legendary English mathematician. Life (not to be confused with the Milton Bradley board game of the same name) permitted the simulation of a wide range of the patterns of the rise and fall and adaptation of living organisms. Using a few simple rules, the game generated a great variety of patterns that were quickly given such colorful names as "snakes," "ponds," "loaves," "beehives," "pulsars," and "overweight spaceships" by aficionados. Although it had originally been played with plastic counters on boards designed for the game of Go, the computer quickly enlarged the scope of Life and the ease with which it is played: ever more complex systems could be built from a relative handful of simple parts. It was a virtual workbook for automata theory, the severe axiomatic discipline that John von Neumann had founded when he began thinking about the parallels between computers and the human nervous system, and it led Albin deep into the most abstract mathematics of basic building blocks. Albin found he could model processes of growth, migration, and decay in economic systems in a way that no General Equilibrium model could offer. The possibilities were obvious, especially since Albin was hip deep in James Meade's seminar on methods of "indicative planning." He foresaw a discipline that would offer answers to the questions: "What makes work complex and meaningful?" and "How can an economy's technical development be planned so that no one is excluded from meaningful and rewarding participation?"

The result was an ambitious book, *The Analysis of Complex Socioeconomic Systems*, published in 1975. The book is almost entirely methodological. It is hard, densely written, confusingly organized, and quite brilliant. It is full of jargon and mathematics, and its author shows little interest in explaining it to persons beyond his immediate circle of peers; he is a scientist, not a journalist. (A second book, *Progress Without Poverty*, which is far more accessible, deals with the mechanisms of technical change and the tendency toward a dual economy that Albin thinks is inherent in an economy in which governments do not oversee production decisions.)

What Albin had in mind in the *Analysis* was comparing the economic order to a computer. He writes: "It is extremely useful to think of the problem of complexity measurement as akin to the problem of describing an advanced IBM 370 System computer in comparison to simpler versions and also in comparison to predecessor models in the 7000 or 650 series. The descriptive parameters (core size, number of relays, number of input/output channels, number of satellite computers, core size of a satellite computer) are analogous to those that would be used to describe the system characteristics of an economy." The point is that complexity exists as a problem in many dimensions: among the important characteristics that had to be taken into account were the range of interactions between individuals or components, the extent of their specialization, the complexity of the individual unit, and the intricacy of the interactions of components. If these qualities could be measured in computing machines, Albin reasons, they could probably be measured in the economic system that built the machines.

The trick was to establish "equivalency classes" of complexity, he said. Borrowing a leaf from Noam Chomsky, the linguist who had classified languages according to complexity, Albin built a system of classes based on units that are machines of varying degrees of sophistication: at the bottom are "primitive" machines, simple binary switches, for example; in the middle are classes corresponding to circuits, algorithms, and microprocessors; at the top, classified as "rich machines" or "loose structures," are classes corresponding to a wide array of complex systems—everything from "jobs requiring analysis" to "jobs requiring synthesis" to "social networks" to "evolutionary systems." It is not an easy system to grasp in its particulars, to put it mildly, but the basic principle is not so hard to understand. "There are things which the higher-class machines can do which the lower-class machines cannot do, no matter how much you extend them," Albin told me one day. "Take an elevator circuit; it has the same basic design whether it is a five-story elevator or a fifty-story elevator, but that design is never going to serve as a microprocessor. You can design a microprocessor to run the elevator for you or to do your taxes, but you can't make the basic elevator circuit do your taxes." Similarly, he said, the important distinction between "mere complication" and "greater complexity" flows from the idea of qualitatively different classes. "Tying one's left shoe and then one's right shoe: that is twice as much complication. Significant increases in complexity come about when you move to one of these richer classes, where there is self-reference, as opposed to a lower level: taking a bath, say." The mathematical theory of equivalency classes has not yet caught up to what are commonsensically distinct classes, Albin says.

"If you ask a typical person to expand on the subject of complexity, you probably find incoherence at some point or another," Albin continues in his *Analysis*. "They say that complexity means 'a lot of things' which seem to be interconnected. There is the aspect of 'interconnection' itself. There is the 'multifaceted' aspect." After a few definitional flourishes, he notes, the effort to be precise about complexity usually runs out of steam—meaning that there is a great research opportunity awaiting the next generation of scholars. He states, "Complexity is as rich a concept as evolution, but in order to use a term like evolution, one must have a great fund of knowledge of the Darwinian mechanisms; it is a term that has meaning because of its associations. With complexity, the issue is to refine and make precise the associations." The only problem, he says, "is that it is hard to be precise."

Albin's professional discussions of measurable complexity, which are full of talk about cellular automata, Turing machines, Godel-richness, and the Krohn-Rhodes decomposition theorem, are already entirely incomprehensible to the layman. I have no intention whatsoever of trying to explain further what he means. After all, this isn't a book about computer architecture. It is enough to say that many of those who have read his book think he is on to something. A teacher in what is surely as obscure a post as any dangerous innovator could desire—the Economics Department at John Jay College of Criminal Justice—he refines his results, achieves small breakthroughs, and concentrates on issues related to work complexity. He has written a new book in the same dense style as his first; *The Structure of Complexity* will be published by Cambridge University Press, probably in 1986. He meets weekly with a small group of disciples who expect that he will turn out to be the Schumpeter of the age.

To Albin's efforts to establish complexity metrics as an analytic and descriptive category in economics, the community of economists has so far responded with a big yawn. Even Herbert Simon, who is no stranger to the analysis of complexity, notes the claim of Albin's *Analysis* to be able to provide measures of socioeconomic complexity, writing, "The economist might react with a 'so what?' " (Most economists will respond to this book in a somewhat angrier fashion, I expect, because of its attempt to place complexity squarely in the context of a major macroeconomic debate—a temptation to overreach that Albin has successfully resisted.)

But there are other analysts of complexity besides Albin. Michael Piore has pursued the connection between technical change and the division of labor with special acuity. Todd LaPorte uses graph theory to depict social complexity, Janos Kornai does institutional analysis of highly structured systems, and Herbert Simon analyzes bounded rationality in evolutionary economic systems. And these are only the three most prominent members in a small but growing community of analysts of complexity in fields related to economics. Whether it is Albin's methods that are finally adopted or those of someone else, the analysis of economic complexity will soon enough become grounded in deep theory. Eventually, the concept will overcome the resistance of economists and find a place near the center of the field. But of course the computer is also the preserve of the expert. For the layman, technical economics is soon going to be harder, not easier, to understand.

7

COMPLEXITY AND FRAGILITY

FOR MANY YEARS, IT WAS AN ARTICLE OF FAITH AMONG ECOLO-gists that stability and complexity went hand in hand. After all, rich tropical systems never seemed to be threatened by the pest outbreaks that ravaged northern climes; simple island systems seemed to accept new species more readily than complicated ones. As Robert M. May says, "Part of the received wisdom of ecology's early days—still to be found in many textbooks—was that complex food webs, with many species interconnected by a tangled maze of strong interactions, tended to be more stable (less affected by natural or man-made disturbances) than simple ones." The idea was that shocks would be more easily muffled and defused in communities in which there were many species, thickly connected, with many interactions.

In the late 1960s and early 1970s, however, this comforting tenet came under fire. A new generation of model-building the-oretical economists began to argue that the opposite might be the case—that as complexity increased, so did the vulnerability of the system to disturbance. Remove a predator from a com-plex system and many other species might vanish too. The model builders showed by their austere logic that stability doesn't automatically follow from complexity. The ecologists then headed back to the field to seek the patterns displayed by real communities.

Something of the same sort has been going on in economics. For many years after World War II, economists congratulated each other on the newfound stability of the international order. There were "built-in stabilizers" in the advanced economies, it was argued, in the form of income taxes and large government budgets that tended to smooth out the the peaks and valleys and lessen the likelihood of another Great Depression. The more enthusiastic analysts proclaimed that the business cycle was dead.

After the bone-jarring recessions of 1974-75 and 1980-83, economists are no longer so sure. There has been a persistent if not exactly growing feeling that the world economic system, in its great new complexity, has become especially vulnerable to shocks and strain. This has much to do with the experience of having lived through the near panics of 1970 (the Penn Central bankruptcy), 1974 (the Franklin National and Herrstadt banks), and 1982 (Drysdale Securities, the Penn Square Bank, and the refinancing of the Mexican national debt). Warnings of great peril came in the early 1980s not from quacks but from serious people, such as Charles Kindleberger, Henry Kaufman, Wassily Leontief, Amory and Hunter Lovins, Felix Rohatyn, Peter G. Peterson, Eliot Janeway, Jay Forrester, and Lester Thurow—all of whom cautioned at one time or another of the danger of imminent collapse.

Just how fragile is a complex economy?

BUSINESS CYCLES

Most arguments about economic fragility begin with the observation that a certain cycle or cycles—a pattern of regular oscillations—seem to be built into the economic system. Then the arguments begin.

The fundamental text on cycles is still Joseph Schumpeter's

two-volume *Business Cycles*, published in 1939. In it he describes a basic, no-frills, three-cycle model, which, he admits, left many things out but which nevertheless seemed to him to serve the purpose. "Five [cycles] would perhaps be better, although after some experimenting, the writer came to the conclusion that the improvement in the picture would not warrant the increase in cumbersomeness," he writes. Schumpeter's approach to cycles was quickly shouldered aside among technical economists by the far more comprehensive and satisfying methods of econometrics. And it lost credibility with the general public when the Depression bottomed out far sooner than Schumpeter had predicted. But it has intellectual charm and a great deal of simplicity to account for its durability, and recent events have returned it to somewhere near center stage. The shape that the three-cycle approach lent to economic history is a sort of Ptolemaic frieze that in formal renditions looks as if it had been laid out above and below a line, using compasses of various sizes.

The three-cycle scheme embraced the Kitchin cycle, as Schumpeter called it, a thirty-nine-month rhythm based on the accumulation of inventories, as the fundamental rhythm of business life. It had been observed more or less simultaneously by two analysts who had published their accounts separately in the January 1923 *Review of Economic Statistics*. Professor W. L. Crum analyzed commercial paper rates in New York from 1866 to 1922 and found forty-month swings; Joseph Kitchin found similar occurrences in bank clearings and wholesale prices both in the United States and England between 1890 and 1922. Kitchin made the bolder claims, so Schumpeter named the cycle for him. Since then, it has become part of the familiar "business cycle" of the elementary economic texts, widely recognized and little debated.

(There was also the Juglar cycle, a seven- or eight-year rhythm based on business investment in plant and equipment, which Schumpeter left out of his three-cycle scheme. He is flattering to the French economist for whom he named this wave, who had made his discoveries during the 1850s. Before Clement Juglar, Schumpeter writes, there had been plenty of writers on "crisis" and "panics" but no clear sense that the seeds of today's events were to be found in the events of yesterday. Juglar's great achievement, according to Schumpeter, is that "he pushed the crisis into the background and . . . discovered below it another, much more fundamental phenomenon, the mechanism of alternating prosperities and liquidations. . . . Henceforth, though it took decades for this new view to prevail, the *wave* ousted the crisis in the role of protagonist in the play.")

Then there was also the Kuznets cycle, a twenty-year rhythm generated by population changes and the construction of new housing that came about as a result of population growth and waves of immigration. Simon Kuznets, who won a Nobel Prize for his creation of the national income accounts, reported the cycle in 1930, and Arthur Burns and Moses Abramowitz helped make it respectable. It received new life and further elaboration from Richard Easterlin, a professor of economics at the University of Pennsylvania who has made a specialty of studying American population growth since World War II.

Finally there was the Kondratieff cycle, which was driven by major technological innovations. This was the famous "long wave," to be named for Nikolai D. Kondratieff, the Soviet economist who, according to Schumpeter, "brought the phenomenon fully before the scientific community and who systematically analyzed all the material available to him on the assumption of the presence of a Long Wave" before dying in the early 1930s in one of Stalin's Siberian labor camps. The first Kondratieff cycle, which began in the 1780s and ended in the 1840s, corresponded to the Industrial Revolution, with the diffusion of steam power and the substitution of machines for human labor, especially in cotton textile manufacturing. The second Kondratieff cycle "stretches over what has been called the age of steam and steel," between 1842 and 1897. "The third, the Kondratieff of electricity, chemistry and motors, we date from 1898 on," Schumpeter writes.

It is of course the Kondratieff wave that has gotten the most attention in recent years. As 1984 loomed, more and more people came forward to announce the end of the "fourth Kondratieff," a long wave associated with pharmaceuticals, synthetic fabrics, plastics, and a variety of other, lesser innovations. Views of the future taken from this vision of the past were heavy with the implication that an inevitable crash was just around the corner in the 1980s. The "secondary depression" of the wave would send prices and production crashing back to levels not seen since the 1930s. Among the most prominent Kondratieff proponents was W. W. Rostow, the economic historian who had touched off an immensely fruitful controversy in the 1950s with his *Stages of Economic Growth*. A particularly dour spokesman for the long wave was MIT's Jay Forrester, an electrical engineer who explained the behavior of the wave as a matter of too much investment, not too little. In Forrester's view, innovations are in some sense incidental to the cycle; the overaccumulation of physical capital is the key. (Forrester's views on the likelihood of depression in the 1980s would have been more influential if his methods hadn't earlier served as the basis for the Club of Rome forecasts in the early 1970s of impending collapse.)

At its most architectonic, the Kondratieff wave has been described by the German economist Gerhard Mensch as a sort of Rube Goldberg contraption in which a mechanical boot is extended to kick scientists in the rear, whereupon they jump up and shout "Eureka." Mensch, now at Case Western Reserve University in Cleveland, argues in *Technology in Stalemate* that innovations appear at the depths of a depression in such a way as to revitalize the economy with the creation of new industries a few years later. Mensch has compiled patent statistics that he says demonstrate a "bunching" of innovations in clusters in each of the crashes that punctuate the Kondratieff expansions:

in the 1760s, the 1820s, the 1880s, and the 1930s. "[In a depression,] reservations about untried, risky new ideas disappear with the sense that relief might come from anywhere," writes Mensch. *Technology in Stalemate* is an extraordinarily interesting and provocative book, but it is very vulnerable to attack because of its implicit conclusion that depressions are good since they cause innovation, for the rate of innovation otherwise tends to stagnate.

Others read the evidence and policy implications of the long wave in just the opposite way: government spending, not crashes, is the best way to stimulate creativity. Christopher Freeman, for example, an influential English social scientist, links research and development with the solution to unemployment. In *Unemployment and Technical Innovation,* he (along with his co-authors, John Clark and Luc Soete) says that it is important to mobilize support for a new "Fifth Wave" now forming. And John Langrish, of the Institute for Advanced Studies at Manchester Polytechnic Institute in England, has gone even further, suggesting that the Kondratieff wave is at least partly a matter of panic and belief. According to a report by David Dickson in *Science*, Langrish says that wishing may help make it so. "If enough people—investors, technologists, designers and such—believe in a coming new age, it will appear sooner through the mechanism of a self-fulfilling prophecy," says Langrish. Count to three and click your heels!

All this is too much for Paul Samuelson, who for forty years has for all intents and purposes been the arbiter of what is serious in economics. He says that all the talk about the long wave is so much "science fiction." Most other mainstream technical economists are skeptical, too. At the 1982 meeting of the American Economic Association (AEA), Nathan Rosenberg and Edwin Mansfield, two of the finest historians of technical change, reported the results of a survey of the Kondratieff wave literature that they made at the request of the AEA's president W. Arthur Lewis. Rosenberg said the evidence for the existence of Kondratieff waves was "far from convincing," and Mansfield declared himself an agnostic in the matter even of the existence of the waves. Wassily Leontieff says, "It is most implausible that over two hundred years a periodicity exists. The whole structure of the economy changes." (To which Jay Forrester retorts that the "fundamental processes underlying the economic long wave have changed very little.")

Obviously, I have a lot of sympathy for the long-wave theorists. Their preoccupation with the "real" side of the economy is laudable. These are the same processes we have seen at work in the history of the division of labor. But for my taste they attempt to do too much, and they attempt the wrong thing. They spend too much time on policy and too little in thinking through the linkages. Patterns of all sorts are interesting, but note that in the long-wave scheme of things, there is still that familiar netting out. Its cycles are like seasons, forever turning back to where they began; whereas with respect to complexity, we are talking about something cumulative, about processes that are depicted by the S curve rather than by the sine wave. It is at a somewhat deeper level that economic complexity operates, as a force that is essentially additive or, in the present case, subtractive.

CAN IT GET STUCK?

The most interesting argument over the vulnerability of the complex modern economic organization concerns whether this cyclical process of the economy is self-correcting or not and, if not, what to do about it. This discussion tends to dwell on the Great Depression, since there has been nothing like it before or since. The real GNP fell by 29 percent between 1929 and 1933; the consumer price index fell by 25 percent; and unemployment rose to 25 percent of the labor force—and stayed high throughout the 1930s. Why was the Depression so deep? Why did it go on so long? John Maynard Keynes, in his 1936 masterpiece, *The General Theory of Money, Interest and Employment*, finds that the economy could get stuck in a "down" position.

Government "pump-priming"—or "demand management," in the language of economists—was therefore a necessity, he argues. The argument has continued ever since.

Another high point in this debate over the need for government intervention in the economy came when Milton Friedman and Anna Schwartz concluded in their 1963 work, *A Monetary History of the United States*—an epic by economic standards—that it was a banking panic, not the stock market crash, that made the Depression great. The huge decline in the quantity of money was what made the contraction so long and painful. "Destroy a country's banking system and the real economy will grind to a halt," says Schwartz. The conclusion was inescapable, write Friedman and Schwartz: monetary policy was only a partner in business cycles, but it was the "senior partner," and the monetary authorities of the Federal Reserve System had allowed it to get out of hand.

Friedman and Schwartz's conclusion was soon challenged by two Keynesian economists, Peter Temin and Charles Kindleberger, who came forward to say that a contraction of the money supply wasn't enough to explain what happened. To Temin, it was a sharp drop in the pattern of consumption and spending that touched off the downward spiral. The recognition of a housing glut contributed to a general unease after 1925, and the collapse of the stock market bubble in October 1929 made things worse. People simply quit spending their money, and banks failed widely as a result. Kindleberger emphasized problems in the international markets as well—including some left over from the peace treaty at Versailles that ended World War I. But he concluded that the Depression became as bad as it did mainly because the United States stood by and did nothing.

At a meeting held in Rochester, New York, in 1978 to discuss the conflicting interpretations of the Depression, intense disputation reigned, and the talk eventually descended into the technical equivalent of the shrug. Temin wondered, "Can the issue of the causes of the Great Depression be fruitfully debated at all?" The monetarist Karl Brunner excoriated, for the usual reasons, the proprietors of the "nonmonetary" explanation of the Great Depression: they were offering too many "little factors" as an explanation instead of one big one, and they couldn't all be right. One wonders whether he would have any more cordially accepted the proposition that the decline in complexity implicit in the "spending hypothesis" of Peter Temin—that it was the decision of a great many people, more or less all at once, to "do without," to sell their houses, liquidate their portfolios, fire the garbageman and bury their garbage in the back yard—had more to do with triggering falling prices than did the decline in the money supply.

Perhaps the most useful purpose of the controversy was to spark Kindleberger to write *Manias, Crashes and Panics.*

WHEN THINGS TURN SOUR

Kindleberger, who was born in 1910, is a modern Walter Bagehot. Though he left his specialty of international economics for what he calls "historical economics" when the international field became highly mathematical in the early 1960s, he retained a knack for being literary and highly technically proficient at the same time. In 1977 Kindleberger set down his thoughts about what made capitalism roll. It was not the business cycle in its entirety with which he was concerned, he writes, but with the moment of turning, with "the final upswing and the initial downturn."

He began with Hyman Minsky, "a man with a reputation among monetary theorists for being particularly pessimistic, even lugubrious, in his emphasis on the fragility of the monetary system and its propensity for disaster." Minksy had been writing since the early 1960s about the built-in instability of the credit system, often in terms that seemed excessively colorful. (The growth of the world economy since World War II was an exercise in "Ponzi finance," he says, dismissing all that economic development by linking it with the name of one of the most imaginative professional swindlers of the twentieth century.) Borrowing the model Minsky had developed for explaining the capitalist system's propensity for disaster, Kindleberger set out to tell the story of the psychology of boom and bust.

In the beginning, some unexpected bit of news ("a displacement") starts things going. A war, a revolution, a recoinage, the appearance of some spectacular new avenue for investment, or some other change of regime occurs; some sudden shift of expectations starts a boom. Soon there is monetary expansion, usually in the form of an increase in bank credit, to fuel the flames. Investors become speculators by borrowing money, Kindleberger says, no matter what that borrowing is imaginatively called. Instability increases. Swindles emerge, a sure sign of the situation's ripening. "Overtrading," the phase is called. What follows is "distress."

"Like overtrading . . . distress is an imprecise term," Kindleberger writes. "It is nonetheless used widely in discussions of financial crises." He catalogued some other words used to describe the interval between the end of euphoria and the onset of crash or panic: "uneasiness," "apprehension," "tension," "stringency," "pressure," "uncertainty," "ominous conditions," and "fragility." More colorful expressions he found include "an ugly drop in the market" and "a thundery atmosphere." He discovered a German metaphor in which the writer describes the "bow being so bent in the fall of 1782 that it threatened to snap."

If the "distress" does not slowly go away—and often it does —what happens next is likely to be a crash, a panic, or both. Either is enough to create a financial crisis. Sometimes it happens rapidly, sometimes slowly, says Kindleberger. Anything can trigger it: a bankruptcy, a suicide, a disappearance, a loan refused, a sudden sale made. But once it starts, it is exceedingly difficult to stop. "Letting it burn out" is the recommendation most frequently offered, but the trouble with such a laissez-faire measure is that the authorities are almost never prepared to stand by and watch the ruin take place. So they try to stop it.

They attempt either to slow things down or to close the market altogether. Banks form committees; governments offer insurance.

But, Kindleberger states, the real medicine for panic is that a "lender of last resort" should step forward, not too soon and not too late, to halt the fear of general ruin with generous loans at penalty rates to failing firms or nations. Over the years, this is the role to which central bankers have become accustomed. When a crisis is international, as almost any twentieth-century crisis must be, the lender of last resort may be the central bank swap network, the Bank for International Settlements or the International Monetary Fund (IMF)—whichever group can operate with the utmost speed and resolution. The book ends with an admirable chart comparing the characteristics of twenty-nine episodes of financial crisis from 1720 to 1975.

I have not done justice to this extraordinary book. It is funny, wise, well informed, and beautifully written, and as a guide to how the system of world trade and finance works, it is a modern equivalent of Bagehot's classic *Lombard Street*. To be sure, by 1984 the international debt situation was much improved. But can anyone fail to recognize the similarity of the international situation that has prevailed for the past three years to the pattern Kindleberger sketches? "Distress" is a term that hardly does it justice. For much of 1982, the situation in the financial centers more nearly resembled a scene from one of those submarine movies in which, during a crash dive to unprecedented depths, sailors listen to the rivets popping one by one. As soon as one sweaty "rollover" negotiation was completed, another with a different debtor nation began. At one point, Brazilian negotiators threw a lavish dinner at New York's Waldorf-Astoria Hotel for officers of the Morgan Guaranty Trust to celebrate an especially difficult bridge loan. Over dessert, the Brazilians mentioned that they would have to defer payment on some of the loan.

Kindleberger's little volume precipitated yet another conference, this time in Germany under the auspices of a prestigious

French think tank, the Maison des Sciences de l'Homme. Hyman Minsky's ideas about the inherent and growing fragility of the system took a terrible beating. Notice was taken of the wide variety of insurance systems, monitoring groups, and reporting requirements that have grown up since the Great Depression to preclude another such crash. The consensus on economic fragility seems to be that economic resilience actually increases with complexity, not the other way around.

But, as Kindleberger warns, the danger remains that "countries will try to shrug the responsibility for international stability off on others." Readers who recall the shameful episode of check dodging in the U.S. Congress over the $8.4 billion supplementary IMF appropriation in late 1983 will recognize that however great our sophistication, the danger of another Great Depression remains.

DISINTERMEDIATION?

Have you noticed that the "fragility" of the economy is not at all what might be meant by a decline in its complexity? It is true that the nearest we come in everyday language to the idea of a decrease in complexity is the idea of a truly deep depression, but implicit in the term is the notion that despite its depth, the economy will somehow snap back. A more interesting case was the condition of the German and Japanese economies following World War II. Suppose the oft-mentioned plan to forbid Germany an industrial sector had been implemented? Surely there would have been a long-term decrease in economic complexity had Germany been reduced to a nation of farmers and kept that way by force of arms.

As growing complexity concerns the growth of knowledge, so does shrinking complexity have to do with the rejection or the supersession of that knowledge. Two philosophers who can help us imagine declining complexity are Ivan Illich and Paul Hawken.

Perhaps the more sweeping vision of diminishing complexity

and what might bring it about is that of Illich. A priest who was trained in social science in Europe before he moved to Cuernavaca, Mexico, Illich is a radical proponent of voluntary simplicity. In a fascinating series of books—including *Deschooling Society, Medical Nemesis,* and *Towards a History of Needs*—he has argued that the "convivial life" requires a systematic rejection of the modern division of labor. Systematic resistance to the vanguard of professional authority—whether that of educators, physicians, managers, or bureaucrats—is the dominant theme of Illich's work, and behind it there is a coherent picture of an alternative world that is more satisfying than any other I know. Not that it is easy to follow. His "politics of conviviality"—meaning "the struggle for an equitable distribution of the liberty to generate use values and for the instrumentation of this production of those industrial and professional commodities that confer on the least advantaged the greatest power to generate value in use"—translates into a celebration of the simple and self-sufficient that sometimes seems to be nothing more than the freedom of Mexican peasants to give birth to their children on their own mats without anyone telling them that it is dirty and dangerous. But as a critic of complexity, Illich time and again comes up with telling insights. If the deflation of money prices is your goal, you could do worse than pursue him, for prices in medicine are not going to go down until the modern medical establishment is rolled up, which Illich at least promises to do peacefully.

Somewhat more down to earth is Paul Hawken, a California tool-company proprietor who is the house economic pundit at the *CoEvolution Quarterly,* a magazine published by the same group that offered *The Whole Earth Catalog.* A couple of times a year, Hawken offers economic advice to the former flower children and others who are his readers. Many of the best pieces have been gathered in a book called *The Next Economy.*

According to Hawken, the world economy is entering a new stage. An "information economy" is replacing a "mass economy"; an age in which mining and manufacturing were dominant is giving way to an age of microelectronics and knowledge. "While the mass economy was characterized by economies of scale, by many goods being produced and consumed by many people, the informative economy is characterized by people producing and consuming smaller numbers of goods that contain more information," writes Hawken. But what is this information? "It is design, utility, craft, durability and knowledge added to mass. It is the quality and intelligence that make a product more useful and functional, longer-lasting, easier to repair, lighter, stronger and less consumptive of energy," he states. For reasons that are never quite clear to me, this is to involve a wholesale retreat from economic complexity. Hawken calls this process "disintermediation."

Originally, disintermediation meant nothing more far-reaching than the illiquidity that resulted when depositors took their money out of low-yielding instruments offered by thrift institutions, causing the housing industry to seize up. But in Hawken's hands, it is used to mean the disappearance of specialized goods, services, and institutions. Thus disintermediation occurs when the consumer begins buying no-frills generic products (out goes the advertising man); when a lawyer writes a how-to-write-your-own-will book; when the "shelf registration" of securities permits companies to bypass their underwriters; and when you pump your own gas or fix your own electric shaver. It isn't necessary to believe, as Hawken does, that "disintermediation is increasing dramatically in every sector of the economy" to recognize that it is a useful term.

In fact, it seems to me that "massive temporary disintermediation" is a pretty good definition of a depression. People fire their suppliers and dump their inventories at losses. They quit their banks and put their money under their beds, after which the banks fail and the bankers go home. Factories shut down. Governments pass laws discouraging international trade and therefore trade dries up. Fleets of tankers are mothballed, crops are unharvested, mines are closed, and factories are locked. In short, the international division of labor collapses and the world returns to a degree of complexity of perhaps a century earlier. Everything gets very, very simple—"simple" being the aspect of life in the Great Depression that is perhaps most frequently singled out by those who remember it. And prices? They fall, of course. Just as growing complexity ordinarily means that basic prices go up, so does declining complexity go hand in hand with falling prices and a contracting money supply—not with mechanical precision, but in line with investors' sentiments.

Hawken's book amounts to a bet that the width, breadth, and depth of the American SIC code is going to shrink. What do you think about that? Will there be fewer than a hundred million jobs in America in 1990? Will the world steel industry really diminish in importance? Perhaps—but only if the plastics industry grows to replace it. Hawken's approach to the next economy has been called "coupon-clipper economics."

A NEW DARK AGE?

What would it take to revert to a world in which farms were worked by hand and messages traveled by mail? What would be required to bring back the nickel beer or to diminish the extent of the division of labor?

How about a default on sovereign debt by Argentina or Poland? Would that do it? It is hard to imagine South American nations continuing to pay 5 percent of their national income on debt service for long, but then it is hard to imagine them opting out of the international system of trade, too (and that, in all likelihood, is what default would entail). The chances are that international debt will be brought back into line, even if it means taking some big losses. How about malice, then? What if the "oil weapon" were deployed or if some other unimagined financial disruption, on the order of the film *Rollover* or the novel *Green Monday*, were to occur? This might shock the system into relative simplicity for a time, but it is hard to imagine what most of its inhabitants would surely regard as a "dark age" being permitted to stand for long. Even big shocks are probably not enough to reduce the world to a truly deep depression. After all, as has been noted, the real point of the Keynesian revolution was that the Great Depression resulted from ignorance too damaging to be borne.

To my mind, the incidents that would achieve a really dramatic decline in the degree of economic complexity are either a nuclear war or some baffling and unstoppable plague. If you like to think about general economic simplicity—and many people do—think of the world one week after a general thermonuclear war. Short of that, there is probably nothing that would turn the clock back very far.

8

CONCLUSION

DURING THE 1960S, *NEWSWEEK* MAGAZINE EMPLOYED A PART-time correspondent, a "stringer," in Gangtok, the capital of the remote Himalayan kingdom of Sikkim. He was an amiable journalist of whom nothing was ever asked but who nevertheless occasionally cabled to New York a dispatch, always on some utterly irrelevant topic, always unbidden, completely out of the blue. One Christmas, for instance, he sent a few hundred words of local color on the holiday scene in the Himalayas. "The oil lamps are lighted in this Sikkimese capital," he began. Another time he cabled, "All Gangtok gripped in grim funk." It was lovely stuff, quite soothing, and much anticipated around the magazine, and it confirmed the reputation of Gangtok as a place where nothing ever happened. Then one day the *Newsweek* teletypes clattered into life with a "press most-urgent" dispatch from Gangtok. "Chinese scientists, working in the mountains north of here, have discovered a new magnetic pole," the stringer cabled. "First reports suggest it may be bigger than the North Pole!"

I confess that at times in the past I have felt a little like that fellow. I have described economic complexity, a new economic

— 178 —

variable, and shown how this concept can augment and even alter our understanding of economic events. In particular, I have argued that the idea of economic complexity may change the way we think about the problem of the rising cost of living by permitting us to see that we are paying for a new and more complex bundle of goods and services (including many quite unrelated to the object of our choice), rather than paying more for the same old things, when we confront higher prices in the marketplace. The process of rising prices is thus seen to involve the full spectrum of human enterprise in the most intimate dialectic with money creation—instead of being a problem of modulation of money supply alone. By treating the traditional subject matter of economics as the history of economic organization—of jobs and work—we develop an entirely different sense of where we have come from and where we are going. Rather than thinking about only GNP per capita, we also measure our journey outward in terms of the increasing differentiation of the work force.

Yet somehow I do not think this quite amounts to suggesting a new pole of thought. Most of the positions I have taken are already intuitively apparent to a vast majority of economists; I have simply sought to put a little more general underpinning beneath what is commonly understood in order to point out the effect of the linguistic grip of monetarism on the debate. Obviously, I do not mean to say that complexity is somehow a bigger or more important concept than supply and demand. It is simply a complementary way of thinking about things. It must exist beside equilibrium analysis, sometimes as a frame for it, sometimes as a footnote. The need for choice among competing uses of scarce resources, about which economics can tell us so much, remains. It is simply that a framework has been added.

Does the frank recognition of the complexity dimension permit some sweeping reformulation of the policy alternatives available to politicians, businessmen, and bureaucrats? Does it open doors that were not open before? Does it make the choices between competing aims simple? Unfortunately, instead it makes them more difficult. I want to survey some of the implications of the views I have presented in this book. I won't say much about them, for these matters need much debate before any firm convictions are justified. There are four broad areas to be noted. They are:

1. Growth: Why does complexity increase?
2. Stabilization policy: How much complexity is enough?
3. Incidence: Who bears the burden of investment in increasing complexity?
4. Life: Personal strategies for coping with complexity.

WHY DO ECONOMIES GROW?

As you might expect, there is among economists a lively debate about the causes of economic growth. Why did the eighteenth-century Industrial Revolution occur when it did? Why did world growth take off so rapidly after World War II? Simon Kuznets learned to measure this growth, Robert Solow learned to model it, Edward Denison sifted through the factors that contributed to it, and many scholars sought to explain it. Mancur Olson, Douglass North, Ester Boserup, W. W. Rostow, and William H. McNeill have all produced serious and widely acclaimed books on the reasons for the rise of nations. Olson lays it to the absence of pressure groups and social rigidity, North to the rise of property rights and the decline of transactions costs, Boserup to population pressures leading to technical change, and Rostow to a "decisive breakthrough" during which "compound interest gets built into society's structure." In a pair of fascinating books, *Plagues and People* and *The Pursuit of Power*, William H. McNeill, a historian at the University of Chicago, looks first at germs (microparasites) and then at warfare (armies viewed as macroparasites) in order to explain some of the abrupt changes in economic organization that have taken place over the past thousand years. His conclusion is that the dangers of the nuclear age may force an end to the widespread use of market capitalism as a mechanism of economic organization and that historians may someday look back "in wonder tinged with awe" at "the reckless rivalries and restless creativity of the millennium of upheaval, A.D. 1000–2000."

I must confess that I like all these explanations of growing complexity and more. As previously noted, from an economist's viewpoint, complexity looks like a deus ex machina, miraculously brought in whenever a change of scene is needed. An economy goes along for a time in one dispensation, there is an explosion of economic complexity as a new sector is added, it levels off, and things settle into a new arrangement and remain there—until another explosion of complexity takes place and another sector is added to the economy. Why? What makes the pattern of increasing complexity resemble a set of stairs? What governs the timing of the "steps"? Well, as I have said, change is difficult; people resist it until somebody—or something—comes crashing through. There must be strong incentives before merchants will risk their lives for gain, before scientists and entrepreneurs will spend their best years locked away during weekends in laboratories and offices. But is this all there is to it? Is it really as simple as the magnitude and structure of the incentives that are offered? My sense of economic history as a whole is that it took the course it did because of countless little things. Some were geographic, some were biological, some were political, some were classically "economic." I simply don't have a strong single theory about why complexity increases.

I do, however, have a couple of observations. One is that economic growth has a lot to do with knowledge. Capital accumulation, the savings rate, and productivity are all important, but growth is more a matter of discovering new opportunities and new ways of organizing them than anything else. Simon Kuznets agrees. "The sustained growth of population and product was made possible by the increasing stock of tested knowledge," he writes. "One might define modern economic growth as the spread of a system of production . . . based upon the increased application of science, that is, an organized system of tested knowledge." There are economists working on an economic theory of the growth of the stock of knowledge; the remarkable Douglass C. North, one of the progenitors of "cliometrics," is among them. Yet I'd put my money on practitioners of the discipline of the history of science to come up with the more valuable insights, year after year.

The other observation is that Western governments have a great deal to do with fostering the growth of economic complexity and that they almost always have. In *Profits from Power*, Frederic C. Lane examines the oceanic expansion of the fifteenth and sixteenth centuries and concludes that from the time of Henry the Navigator and Columbus to the colonial enterprises that followed—the early years of the world economy— it was nearly impossible to separate "business" from "government" enterprise. "Only after the use of force was applied in a colonial area in a way favorable to economic development was business organized into enterprises distinct from the organization of government," Lane writes. From the Venetian armories to the joint stock companies, he notes, public finance and the private division of labor have gone hand in hand.

This connection is especially clear in the rise of the computer industry. The first large digital computer was built under contract to the U.S. Army, and most of the early engineering development of computing machines was done by firms with strong government connections. As late as 1954, the International Business Machines Corporation (IBM) was still debating internally whether to get out of the computer business altogether for lack of sufficient opportunities to make money. Perhaps only the Air Force's contract for its SAGE (Semi-automatic Ground Environment) air defense system kept IBM in, for during the 1950s, more than half of IBM's domestic computing revenues came from its SAGE contract and some work on B-52 bombers undertaken in connection with the Korean War, according to the history of the firm produced in connection with its antitrust defense. "Without the stimulus provided by these large federal contracts," conclude the authors, "the early growth of IBM business would have been significantly slower."

My colleague Jonathan Kaufman has called attention to the similar way in which the Kennedy administration's commitment to the space race led, by a series of fairly direct steps, to the rise of the semiconductor industry. Writing in the *Wall Street Journal*, Kaufman noted that while everybody remembers the men on the moon, "NASA also poured more than $20 billion into the computer, semiconductor and aerospace industries. It assumed much of the risk for long-term research and development and encouraged close cooperation between business and government. It dispensed funds to a wide variety of companies, providing seed money for new ventures as well as bolstering established giants." In other words, he concludes, NASA behaved just like MITI, the Japanese Ministry of Industry and Trade that is often held up as the model of industrial planning. (Kaufman doesn't note—but he could have—that the same thing can be said of the Atomic Energy Commission's drive into nuclear power, using Navy submarines as research vehicles and electrical utilities as often unwilling dragoons. How you feel about industrial planning will influence which example you choose.)

What we are dealing with here has far more in common with the world envisaged by Fernand Braudel than that envisaged by Milton Friedman. Friedman sees quick, machine-like adjustments, economic actors all pursuing their rational self-interests at all times. Braudel sees long slow changes, a topography in which change takes place mainly at the pinnacle. Braudel's is a world of hierarchies that start with the humblest jobs and lead all the way up to the great committees of the multinational corporations. Time and again, close studies of these chains demonstrate that at their top, the public and private realms are often nearly indistinguishable—as described, for example, in David Landes's brilliant study of the history of the timekeeping industry or Alfred Chandler's meticulous chronicle of the invention by the Du Pont company of that mainspring of modern corporations, the executive committee, in the shadow of World War I.

The theology derived from Adam Smith—that the market and only the market can be relied upon to dictate the need for specialization—is not only morally wrong, it is analytically inferior. Allyn Smith was right: increasing returns are the secret of economic growth, and the extent of the market is determined by the division of labor as often as the reverse situation. What, then, determines the extent of the division of labor in these cases? The answer is management—in Alfred Chandler's phrase, "the visible hand." The broadening of the market often proceeds in a very intimate dialectic between the public and private sectors. My own feeling is that government should concentrate on keeping the physical plant in good shape, on running the schools, on maintaining the army—and on taking an occasional big flyer on some generally agreed-upon end. That old chestnut about Teflon for frying pans being the only good thing to come out of the space race is clearly wrong. We owe a good deal of the electronics age to our Cold War competition with the Russians. Government spending is often a terrific goad to economic growth—the problem is that it would be good to know exactly when!

WHAT ABOUT "INFLATION"?

On October 5, 1979, Paul Volcker stepped before the microphones at the offices of the Board of Governors of the Federal Reserve System to announce what seemed to be a relatively minor change. The board was going to target and attempt to control monetary aggregates instead of interest rates, he said. It was going to clamp down on the money supply.

Not many were prepared for the severity of the four-year recession that ensued. Output dropped precipitously, growth stopped, and unemployment soared, but sure enough, "inflation" stopped dead in its tracks—at least for a couple of months. First the silver and gold bubbles burst, then the real-estate fever cooled, and finally oil prices fell. The world economy teetered on the brink of a crushing depression, then seemed to back away from the edge. Prices began creeping up again, but at a far lower rate than before.

What did the experiment prove? (Remember, "inflation" had been the central topic of concern in certain circles for twenty-five years.) Well, some said it proved that the monetarists had been right all the time. After all, hadn't it happened in just the way the theory had led them to expect? Monetarists always said that if the rate of growth of the money supply were reduced sharply, the rate of "inflation" would fall. Others said that the Phillips Curve looked pretty good in retrospect: with its trade-off between full employment and rising prices, it had always indicated bottlenecks in the labor market to be the principal sources of "inflation." With a lot of people out of work, the reasoning goes, those who keep their jobs won't be so quick to ask for raises, and the rate of wage change—and eventually price rise—will come down. Still others told a story about how America "regained its nerve." Everything had been fine with the world economy until Lyndon Johnson blew it off course with his guns and butter policy on Vietnam; then OPEC stepped in and mucked things up further. In this version, a gallant Volcker stepped in to get the world back on track.

Naturally I believe that each of these explanations contains only a piece of the truth—that what happened in the 1980-82 recession and later was somewhat more fundamental than any of these three interpretations suggest. My hunch is that two other key events leading to the relative economic calm of the 1980s were the tax revolt of the 1970s—a decision on the part of voters in Europe, Great Britain, and the United States to rein in the growth of government, which amounted to an attempt to halt a Type B revolution that had been building for fifty years —and a change in technology that may amount to a Type A revolution. The spectacular cost savings associated with computer-based techniques for management and control have the flavor that characterized inventions whose speedy diffusion accompanied the ages of level prices in our *tour d'horizon*.

Meanwhile, many other sorts of cost-decreasing complexity were coming into existence, thanks to the broadening of the world market and the growing complexity of world trade. International competition in steel, television sets, and cars put a downward pressure on prices, and there were many other factors at work that involved the complexity of the international division of labor. But the basic impulse, I suspect, was the turn away from a movement toward the "public" that had begun in the 1880s and gathered steam in the 1940s. A great economic revolution was winding its way to completion; the "mixing" of the economies of the world was finally complete. In combination with the end of government's Big Push, the computer may lead to an era of (almost) stable prices. It was this tide that Paul Volcker's tight money caught and turned to advantage; the rate of price increase was cut in half. It may decline considerably further by the end of the decade.

It is in this sense that the world debt crisis should be understood. The crunch attendant on the refinancing of the Mexican debt that loomed so suddenly in the summer of 1982 (and has continued like a low-grade fever ever since) is a side effect of a world whose financial rules shifted suddenly from one dispensation to another. Speculation about bank failures in the United States resulting from offshore defaults, which enlivened many a newspaper column for a year, came to naught; it was clear that the government would take whatever steps were necessary to ensure that dollar liabilities would be met. Bankers adopted every sort of artifice to make sure that that "workouts" and "rollovers" would succeed, and that the institutional features of the "new" world would resemble those of the "old."

Whatever the case, it is important to understand that the talk about "targeting monetary aggregates" instead of interest rates was almost strictly diversionary. As Leonard Silk has observed, the tactic "permitted the Fed and other central banks to deal a harder blow to the economy with the uppercut of higher interest rates than would have otherwise been possible. Governments could act innocent of any intention to raise interest rates and to dump the economy to cure inflation." However the Fed explained its action, it had simply decided to put the economy into a stall, and very high interest rates were the means for doing this. The success of the Fed in contriving a deep and prolonged world recession doesn't "validate" or "bear out" the view of the world implied by the Quantity Theory of Money, however, any more than would the failure of the banker to pass out money to Go-passers in the game of Monopoly. The point of the game in the real world, as in Monopoly, is to grow more complex, not to keep prices level.

The message of the 1980 election and that of subsequent events seems to me to have been a ratification of Volcker's decision. The election suggested that people are willing to forgo quite a lot of growth in order to bring prices under control. More than anything else, a swing toward public austerity may turn out to have been responsible for the decline in the rate of rising prices, mainly through an easing of the pressure on the cost side. A willingness to tolerate the extremely tight money was part and parcel of the change in mood.

As for slowing "inflation" further, there is a wide menu of midrange policies of the sort that David Stockman and Martin Feldstein excel at developing. Henry Kaufman has a list of banking reforms that, if instituted, would considerably diminish the fragility of the newly deregulated financial sector. These measures are not the stuff of headlines, but they are exceedingly important and, if adopted, would add up to a lower rate of price increase. The Democrats must learn to love the market; if they don't, they will be beaten badly again and again. The Republicans must learn to exercise the latent powers of government, to behave like grownups. Paul Volcker must be bold one day and cautious the next, and he already knows that.

It is useful to remember that the man who gave us the policy goal of no "inflation" whatsoever was a Yale professor named

Irving Fisher. A diet faddist, he came to economics from physics, having been trained by the great physicist Willard Gibbs. For his dissertation, Fisher built a great hydraulic machine to demonstrate principles of general equilibrium. He had Boyle's Law in his head and an ozone machine crackling away at his feet as he wrote. (The oxygen radical was supposed to be good for the brain.) The "stable money movement," as Fisher calls it, was only one of his public causes. His other great enthusiasm was Prohibition. Indeed, he may be responsible for the pervasive analogy between creeping "inflation" as a social problem and alcoholism. Perhaps a gradual increase in prices must be tolerated, says this analogy, as long as it doesn't get out of hand; perhaps gently rising prices should come to be considered an uncomfortable side effect of modernity, likely to be with us for a long time, but far from the main ring of policy. An attempt to get rid of it altogether might cost far more than it is worth.

On the other hand, the message of the Phelps Brown data seems to be that there may be long "zones" of stable prices built for one reason or another into human history. If this is so, and if the reasons for this can be agreed upon, then we should not fail to attempt to take advantage of the opportunities that come our way for reducing the rate of "core inflation" to zero. There are larger schemes for halting the momentum of rising prices that are intriguing and should be studied. What about Thomas Sargent's frequent citation of the European nations' experience in stopping "hyperinflation" after World War I? Can you reduce the "core rate" of "inflation" merely by saying "persuasively" that you really mean to stop it? (I trust this strong form of the "rational expectations" hypothesis has already been discarded.) What about a Jacques Rueff–style devaluation—knock a zero or two off every price—just to underscore a national commitment to prices expressed in numbers that children can manipulate? Even Irving Fisher's plan for a commodity-backed dollar, recently dusted off by the economist Robert Hall, deserves close scrutiny, especially now that we seem to be in calmer times. But these schemes should be approached with great care. The kind of call-in of big bills advocated by the consultant James Henry—in which the government would swap "new series" $100 bills for old ones in order to catch the crooks who have more $100 bills than they can explain—is an appalling idea. It is not play money we are talking about, it is an artifact second in importance only to language.

For precisely this reason, therefore, I beleve that the very dramatic, even risky steps that were taken in 1979 to 1983 to slow the core, or "pass-along," rate of "inflation" were worthwhile. The world has become one in which sums expressed in money must be constantly multiplied or divided in order to have meaning. There is no simple way to convey the widespread sense of unease that fifty years of rising prices has engendered, but the experience had no better chronicler than *New York Times* columnist Russell Baker. In one memorable column, for example, Baker writes, "As a child of the Great Depression, I have never recovered from the illusion that a dollar is money. Fifty dollars to me still speaks of the wealth of the Indies. Intellectually, I know better. Obviously a single dollar nowadays is trash. Psychologically, though, I remain unable to accept the death of the dollar. When OPEC destroyed it a few years ago, I withdrew from the marketplace entirely. Quit going to the grocery. Always handed my wallet to somebody else when we got to the box office and said, 'You buy the tickets, but don't tell me how much they cost.' " Baker claims that the years of deliberately avoiding contact with the price of things have left him bewildered: "I haven't the remotest notion of what is a sensible price to pay," he writes. A few years later, he says, when he resumed trying to do his own shopping, the dollar had been replaced by little plastic cards. "Thus I was able to buy three or four presents before I felt the breakdown coming on. The gifts include a quart of anti-freeze, a bottle of foot-bath bubble lotion and a key ring. I'm not sure what I bought after that. The sudden thought that the key ring might cost anything between $1.98 and $7,000 left me too faint to pay attention to what happened next."

Russell Baker's pain was real. People cannot take it. It is time to stop.

WHO BEARS THE BURDEN?

A particularly troubling question about complexity arises when we ask, "Who pays for progress?" That is, assuming that the cost of creating new sectors isn't evenly shared, who suffers and how much? What we want is an index of purchasing power of wages over time for different groups of people in particular economies. We may see who suffers, and then we may ask if it has anything to do with the revolution.

One such indicator is Ray DeVoe's Cost-of-Living-It-Up Index. DeVoe, a Wall Street analyst who writes a newsletter for his firm's customers, has for some years kept track of the price of a basket of luxury goods: a year at Harvard, a necktie from Dunhill's, a champagne cocktail at New York's "21" Club, a pair of front row seats on Broadway, and so on. His conclusion is that rising prices have been tough on rich people. Or, as a du Pont family member put it after watching the Robert Redford version of *The Great Gatsby*, which had been filmed in Newport, "A lot of good things went out with the income tax." The sort of life portrayed in the upstairs half of *Upstairs, Downstairs* is now priced so high that almost no one can afford it.

On the other hand, such wage data as we have for the average worker make his experience in the United States look dazzling. With the exception of the Great Depression, the working American has done fine throughout the century. Per capita income has risen steadily and the average real personal disposable income (i.e., after-tax wages) has gone from around $2,200 a year in 1948 to more than $4,500 a year in 1978 (measured in 1972 dollars). Paid vacations, which were virtually nonexistent in the 1920s, are today nearly universal. So the moral seems to be that something of a leveling off has taken place. Scholars of income and wealth distribution aren't sure of it, but the evidence tends to support the view that "upstairs" and "downstairs" have moved a little closer together. What the "Reagan revolution" did to the distribution of income—and it probably did plenty—remains to be seen. But for the present, anyway, they are not building those grand houses anymore.

It is only when we look at the long sweep that doubts arise. Again, the most interesting evidence on the subject is to be had from E. H. Phelps Brown and Sheila V. Hopkins. This time it is their comparison of the purchasing power of the wages of a carpenter and his helper over time.

First Phelps Brown and Hopkins studied wages over a period of seven centuries. (One of their remarkable findings was that average money wages in southern England actually fell only three times in that period: during the Great Depression, during the short, sharp Depression of 1921, and in the 1330s. "Sticky wages" were thus not something invented by unions!) Then they compiled their price index and compared prices with wages. The result, an estimate of the real purchasing power of the craftsman's wage. is shown in Figure 10.

The salient features are the two big drops. From a high in 1500, real income falls over the course of the sixteenth century to a quarter of what it had been at the beginning. Starting in about 1650, it begins to climb again until, beginning in about 1750, it is again knocked back down. It isn't until 1880 that the real wage of a representative carpenter regains the level at which it had stood when Henry VIII was crowned. These are events of astonishing magnitude and import; it is hard to imagine what the modern worker's response would be to such a decline in the standard of living.

Since the collapses of real wages coincide with the onset of price explosions, we may surmise that economic revolutions are impoverishing, either through a Malthusian mechanism or in some other way. In any event, this appears to be a graphic picture of the "imiseration" of the workers, as described in Marx-

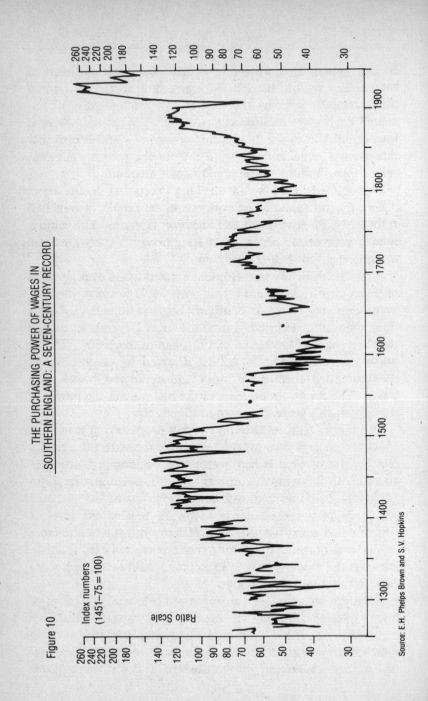

Figure 10

THE PURCHASING POWER OF WAGES IN
SOUTHERN ENGLAND: A SEVEN-CENTURY RECORD

Index numbers
(1451–75 = 100)

Ratio Scale

Source: E.H. Phelps Brown and S.V. Hopkins

ist theory, and as good a reason as any for the working class to harbor a continuing grudge. Did the fall in wages really take place? Not surprisingly, economic historians cannot agree, although they have conducted extensive debates (if not much research) on the matter. But the mere fact that so scarring an experience might have been the lot of most Englishmen in the twin dawns of the capitalist and industrial systems is sufficient to arouse our interest.

When we look for a similar episode of imiseration in England in the course of the twentieth-century price explosion, we find none. After World War II, there is some slight falling off from previous peaks in real wages, but by 1954, when the Phelps Brown index ends, the real wage has begun to gain again, and it has been climbing ever since—at least until Thatcher's government took office. Meanwhile there has been a general tightening of the wage pattern. The gap that existed for centuries between the skilled tradesman and his unskilled helper has all but disappeared in the Phelps Brown data. This time the revolution wore a smile—or did it?

It is facile to repeat that the undeveloped nations have become the "country" of the world economy while the industrial nations are its "cities," but there is nevertheless a great truth in this cliché about the burgeoning complexity of the international order. The point is that in a world system, the only interesting statistics in income distribution will be global ones: to measure the dispersion of wages in England and the United States alone is like looking at incomes in the New York City suburbs of New Rochelle, Scarsdale, and Bronxville while forgetting about the boroughs of Brooklyn, Queens, Staten Island, and the Bronx.

What one wishes for, therefore, are comparable series on real wages over a long period of time for Third World workers. The decline in real standards of living in much of the Third World that has taken place since OPEC took hold is indisputable. If the Third World has been front-ending the investment for the growth of industrial complexity in the oil-exporting nations, we should know about it—and so should they. It may be true, as

Rostow says, that over time, the rich slow down and the poor catch up; it may even be that this occurs most efficiently through the sort of mechanism represented by OPEC. But we should do what we can—which is quite a lot—to reduce the long and painful lags, largely by encouraging world trade. We should see the problem as a whole.

There is another problem here, one concerning the standoff between the industrial democracies and the communist world. The gap between the standard of living in the West and behind the Iron Curtain grows greater every day. There are twenty-six centrally planned economies, in which almost 40 percent of the world's population lives. Together they produce slightly less than 20 percent of the world's gross domestic goods, of which a disproportionate part—around 13 percent of the GNP—goes for military spending. It adds up to 40 percent of the world total for arms. (In contrast, the United States spends between 5 and 7 percent of its GNP on arms.) The prospect for the knitting together of these two blocs through extensive foreign trade is not bright. Can two quite different systems really coexist peacefully when the gap between them—material and technical—grows greater every day? Given the exceedingly precarious balance of the arms race, it seems to me that all the questions really worth worrying about grow out of this great inequality.

WHAT ARE THE PROSPECTS?

The historian Carlo Cippola once said that there are two great dividing lines in human history: the agricultural revolution that occurred around 800 B.C., when men became farmers, and the Industrial Revolution, when they learned to manipulate nature. A somewhat higher resolution lens is supplied by Daniel Bell, who describes the "post-industrial" world as the age of the meeting, the office having replaced the smokestack as the symbol of the age. How does economic complexity affect you? How will you fare in the twenty-first century? This depends, naturally, upon who you are and on your specialty.

The average person probably doesn't need to think very much at all about complexity. Most of the hundred million U.S. jobs are relatively safe. In fact, all the high tech growth and international competition are not really cutting away the agricultural and industrial core as much as the headlines suggest; instead, they are growing up around it. The service sector has grown to around 60 percent of civilian employment, and industrial employment has stayed relatively steady since the turn of the century, having fallen to 36 percent today from a 1950 high of 42 percent. Agricultural employment has declined from 47 percent of the work force a hundred years ago to 3 percent today—but that scarcely means that America is a nation without farms. It is possible, but not likely, that the industrial sector will show a similar decline in the next fifty years. Even industries that we talk about as if they had died because they stopped growing, such as nuclear power, continue to do business, if not to thrive.

For the businessman and policy maker, there is much to be said for Theodore Levitt's approach: strive continually to stick to simple methods of management. Complex management tools have often led to trouble in both socialist economies and in the West, says Levitt. They are taught in America in graduate schools of business management, mostly by "social-climbing technocrats who pretend with increasing vigor to dispense grace and salvation [and who] have infiltrated the crevices of weakness and self doubt," Levitt says, and many a would-be corporate titan has come to grief using the latest heavily mathematical technique for asking "what if" questions. "Even if business is getting more complex, as many people claim, it doesn't follow that the organizational structures of today's companies have to be more involuted, planning more rigid and detailed, control systems more elaborate, or decision-making more cumbersome and scientific," Levitt writes. "There is only one way to manage anything, and that is to keep it simple."

Those who do serious research in economics and those who sponsor it would do well to recognize that this profession is just one of the many social sciences that can provide a better under-standing of the workaday world. The fields that have grown up on the periphery of technical economics seem especially prom-ising as they extend their aims and influence. Systems analysts, historians, regional scientists, sociologists, anthropologists, and engineers all have something to say about the matters now thought to be the special province of economics. These intellec-tual skirmishes will probably be one of the best continuing sto-ries in the social sciences in the next twenty years.

As for money management, we have seen that the meaning of "inflation" is that you can't relax. There are too many people trying to get you to help pay for their living. Well, who wants to live life in a time like that of Balzac? Then you relax too much, for if you have money there is almost no way to lose it, and if you do not have it there is almost no way to make it. William McNeill says that "it is easy to imagine a time not far in the future when existing public and private bureaucracies might come together into a self-perpetuating structure aimed first and foremost at keeping things as nearly stable as possible by guard-ing the privileges and power of existing managerial elites around the globe. If this should happen, market regulated be-havior will swiftly be cribbed, cabined and confined to the in-terstices of society." Somehow I doubt it. Now that Sears is branching into financial services, now that you can place a bet on the stock market with the ease with which you used to pick up a monkey wrench, I suspect that market-governed special-ization is here to stay, and that therefore individual investors had better sharpen up their skills, at least in choosing mutual funds.

Certainly managers and the people who consult them should be alert to issues of work complexity. There is more than one reason for considering job richness and productivity to be linked. If Japanese and Scandinavian auto manufacturers can obtain a significant cost advantage by minimizing precisely those features of the assembly line that workers find objection-able and by making work more complex, then there is also a great deal of room for improvement in other realms of work. Shared control of work promises other sorts of efficiency. "There isn't going to be any more 'I'm the boss, you're the horse,' " says an executive at a steel company quoted in a magazine. Some of the most interesting work that crosses my desk has to do with corporate managers and others who are finding ways to increase the sense of efficacy and participation of individual workers in large organizations.

If you are a young person starting out, the best advice would seem to be to immerse yourself in complexity. Become comfortable with it. Study it. Learn to manipulate it, to dive down in it and to come up with something simple—but not too simple. Recognize that once you fall behind in mathematics and foreign languages, there is no catching up. True, you can live a life of ease, of voluntary simplicity, more easily today than at many times in the past. You may be suited to it. But if you aren't, it won't be much fun, whereas the satisfactions of doing real work are very great.

There is a widespread feeling that somehow the complexity of modern life has gotten out of hand, that it now threatens to overwhelm us. I don't think so; to me, more complex means richer and better. But then, certain human requirements remain the same whatever the complexity of the living world. Finding personal simplicity in the modern age isn't easy, but it remains the most important human task.

FURTHER READING AND REFERENCES

AMONG THE MATERIALS I CONSULTED IN THIS REPORTING PRO-
ject were the books and magazine articles cited below; the list
isn't meant to be exhaustive, but rather to be indicative of the
kinds of materials upon which I depended. Professionals who
wish to pursue these topics will quickly find their way to the
primary sources. It is inevitable that I have neglected to credit
the sources of some views; I hope that the omissions are few
and insignificant.

PREFACE

The articles in which I first broached the book's themes were:
"Is Depression the Only Cure for Inflation?" *Forbes*, March 1,
1975; "How Much Should the Government Take?" *Forbes*, October 15, 1975; "Inflation Is Too Important to Leave to the
Economists," *Forbes*, November 15, 1976; and "The Great
Hamburger Paradox," *Forbes*, September 15, 1977. An unsuccessful but highly useful iteration was published in a series of
five articles in the *Boston Globe*, on May 28, June 4, June 11,
June 18, and June 25, 1979. It was only when I wrote a profile

of Peter Albin that the material jelled in its present form: this was entitled "Complexity . . . from a Game" and appeared in the *Boston Globe*, June 2, 1981, p. 33. *Honky Tonk*, the delightful 1941 movie I quoted in the 1976 article, was directed by Jack Conway and written by Marguerite Roberts and John Sanford; in fact, I misquoted it; after the publication of the article, I discovered that Gable actually says, "What do they mean they can't pay more *rent*?" However, it seems to me that this confusion of cost headings underscores my original point.

INTRODUCTION

The business of economics is mainly recorded in technical journals. Therefore, I've done what any journalist would do: looked at half a dozen of the leading economic journals for treatments of complexity, and though I certainly can't read the most technical articles, I'm reasonably certain that in the past half century, *The American Economic Review*, *The Economic Journal*, *The Journal of Political Economy*, *The Quarterly Journal of Economics*, *The Review of Economic Studies*, and *Economica* contain no direct treatment of the fundamental issues that are raised here. I also searched the *Journal of Post-Keynesian Economics* and the *Journal of Economic Issues;* and while complexity is implicit in much that is done by the "institutionalist" economists who publish in these journals, straightforward treatments are not to be found. Indeed, in all of the mainstream literature, the closest thing I've discovered to an unambiguous consciousness of what is meant by "economic complexity" is Douglass C. North's aside in *Structure and Change in Economic History* to the effect that "while historical statistics are not organized to specifically mirror specialization and the division of labor, the changing proportion of blue collar (production) workers to white collar workers gives some indication" (p. 176). I cannot mention the consensus of technical economics without singling out the two basic maps of it that have served me and millions of others so well: Paul Samuelson's *Economics* and Robert Heilbroner's *The*

Worldly Philosophers. It is the theory of economics and the history of this theory, as spelled out with extraordinary clarity in these volumes, with which this volume is concerned.

1. THE DISCOVERY OF COMPLEXITY

Warren Weaver's remarks may be found in "Science and Complexity," *American Scientist* 36 (1948); Herbert Simon's thoughts are collected in *The Sciences of the Artificial.* Friedrich von Hayek's essay, "The Theory of Complex Phenomena," is in his *New Studies in Philosophy, Politics, Economics and the History of Ideas.* For an especially suggestive treatment of the idea of complexity in another sphere, consult Robert Venturi, *Complexity and Contradiction in Architecture.* Complexity is a hot topic among ecologists; an introduction is Stuart L. Pimm, *Food Webs.* The Dayak incident, cited in Amory and Hunter Lovins's *Brittle Power,* was reported in C. S. Holling and M. A. Goldberg, "Ecology and Planning," in the *Journal of the American Institute of Planners,* July 1971. The attitude toward creation that is called plenitude is delineated in Arthur O. Lovejoy, *The Great Chain of Being,* and discussed in Stephen Toulmin and June Goodfield, *The Discovery of Time.* The rise of information theory is gracefully described in Jeremy Campbell, *Grammatical Man,* and a more difficult but also rewarding account is Steve J. Heims, *John von Neumann and Norbert Wiener: From Mathematics to the Technologies of Life and Death.* The development of automata theory is described in *Essays on Cellular Automata,* edited by A. W. Burks. Problems of chip design and computational complexity have been reported in various articles in *Science,* including "Are VLSI Microcircuits Too Hard to Design?" 209, July 11, 1980. The quotation on microcircuit potentials is from Stan Augarten's excellent *State of the Art, A Photographic History of the Integrated Circuit.* With regard to code-cracking, see, for example, "Cryptography, A New Clash Between Academic Freedom and National Security," by Gina Kolata, in *Science* 209, August 29, 1980. Oscillating reactions are discussed in "Oscillating Chemical Reactions" in *Scientific American* for March 1983. The implications of physical complexity are discussed in Ilya Prigogine, *From Being to Becoming: Time and Complexity in the Physical Sciences*, and in Eric Jantsch, *The Self Organizing Universe*. Prigogine's 1977 Nobel Prize in chemistry was described in *Science* 198, November 25, 1977. An English translation of Prigogine's and Isabelle Stenger's widely circulated book *Order out of Chaos, The Evolutionary Paradigm and the Physical Sciences* was finally scheduled to be published in the United States in early 1984.

2. THE IDEA OF ECONOMIC COMPLEXITY

For a particularly vivid sense of what has changed in this century in America and England, see Daniel Boorstin, *The American Experience*, volume 3, and Bruce Chatwin, *On the Black Hill*. Samples of orthodox approaches to complexity can be found in *Approaches to the Study of Social Structure*, edited by Peter M. Blau; Daniel Bell, *The Coming of Post-Industrial Society;* George Park, *The Idea of Social Structure;* Nathan Rosenberg, *Inside the Black Box: Technology and Economics;* Kelvin Lancaster, *Variety, Equity and Efficiency;* Dan Usher, *The Measurement of Economic Growth;* and Ian M. D. Little, *Economic Development*. A disappointing book is Maurice N. Richter, Jr., *Technology and Social Complexity*. An explication of John Hicks's idea of the Impulse can be found in his essay on "Industrialism" in his *Economic Perspectives*. Classic statements on the division of labor are found in Plato's *Republic;* Adam Smith, *The Wealth of Nations;* Alexis de Tocqueville, *Democracy in America;* Emile Durkheim, *The Division of Labor in Society;* Karl Marx, *Das Kapital*, especially volume 1, chapters 12-15 and 26-32; and in Max Weber, *Economy and Society*, part 3, chapters 3, 4, 6 and 9. See also Arthur Salz's superbly suggestive essay, "Specialization," in the first edition of *The International Encyclopedia of the Social Sciences* and a perverse but lively essay by Stephen A. Marglin, "What Do Bosses Do? The Origins and Function of

Hierarchy in Capitalist Production," in the *Review of Radical Political Economics* 6, no. 2, Summer 1974. *Readings in the Theory of Growth*, edited by Frank Hahn, contains most of the significant papers in the mainstream economics of growth. Allyn Young's Presidential Address was published in the *Economic Journal* for December 1928; two interesting treatments of Young are an essay by Charles P. Blitch, "Allyn Young: A Curious Case of Professional Neglect," *History of Political Economy*, volume 15, number 1; and Nicholas Kaldor, "The Irrelevance of Equilibrium Economics," in the *Economic Journal*, December 1972. *The Standard Industrial Classification Manual*, Government Printing Office, 1972, is the basic source on the SIC code; a slim update was published in 1977. Ann P. Carter, *Structural Change in the American Economy*, is a useful companion. Technical writing on economic complexity includes Peter Albin's two books: *The Analysis of Complex Socioeconomic Systems* (1975) and *The Structure of Complexity* (forthcoming). Examples of various ways in which the history of the division of labor may be written are Thomas L. Haskell, *The Emergence of Professional Social Science;* Alfred Chandler, *The Visible Hand: The Managerial Revolution in American Business;* Fernand Braudel, *Capitalism and Material Life;* and Thomas Kuhn, *The Structure of Scientific Revolutions*. It is interesting to compare the account of hog butchering in Upton Sinclair's *The Jungle* with the account given in "Modern Pork Production," in *Scientific American* for May 1983.

3. COST WEBS AND EVERYDAY PRICES

The similarity between defense and medical economics has been little noticed by economists. The best analysis of the health care problem is Martin Feldstein's *Hospital Costs and Health Insurance;* there seems to be nothing similar on the economics of preparing for war. Descriptions of particular cost webs may be found in David Halberstam, *The Breaks of the Game;* Paul Starr, *The Social Transformation of American Medi-*

cine; James Fallows, *The National Defense;* Mary Kaldor, *The Baroque Arsenal;* Fred Kaplan, *The Wizards of Armageddon;* Seymour Melman, *Pentagon Capitalism;* Anthony Sampson, *The Arms Merchants;* Robert Sherrill, *The Oil Follies of 1970- 1980: How the Petroleum Industry Stole the Show (And Much More Besides);* Robert Caro, *The Power Broker;* Lewis Mumford, *The City in History: Its Origins, Its Transformations and Its Prospects;* Jane Jacobs, *The Death and Life of Great American Cities;* Marvin Harris, *America Now;* and Martin Mayer, *The Bankers.* An introduction to the technical literature on the "index number problem"—that is, on the difficulty of measuring the purchasing power of money over time—may be found in William A. Gale, "How Well Can We Measure Price Changes?" in a book he edited, *Inflation: Causes, Consequen*ces *and Control.* Also interesting is Jack E. Triplett, "The Measurement of Inflation, A Survey of Research on the Accuracy of Price Indexes," in *The Analysis of Inflation,* edited by Paul Earl. The technical literature on the "direction of causation" problem includes much that is unfathomable. Good starting points are Chrisopher Sims, "Money, Income and Causality," *American Economic Review,* 1972, which started the debate, and his article "Exogeneity and Causal Ordering" in *New Methods in Business Cycle Research,* published by the Federal Reserve Bank of Minneapolis. None of this controversy over statistical inference is very accessible to the lay reader.

4. THE COMPLEXITY HYPOTHESIS I

Good introductions to the framework and vocabulary with which economists analyze "inflation" are Robert Solow, "The Intelligent Citizen's Guide to Inflation," in *The Public Interest* 38, 1975; James Tobin, "Inflation," in *The McGraw-Hill Dictionary of Economics: A Handbook of Terms and Organizations,* 2nd ed.; and John Case, *Understanding Inflation.* An introduction to price history is found in William Beveridge, *Prices and Wages in England from the 12th to the 19th Century;* E. H. Phelps

Brown and Sheila V. Hopkins, *A Perspective of Wages and Prices;* Fernand Braudel and Frank Spooner's essay "Prices in Europe from 1450 to 1750," in *The New Cambridge Economic History of Europe,* volume 4; and *The Price Revolution in Sixteenth Century England,* edited by Peter Ramsey. An excellent history of English money over the millennium is the second edition of A. E. Feavearyear's *The Pound Sterling.* For illuminating discussions of the long-term trend of prices, see Anna Schwartz, "Secular Price Change in Historical Perspective," *The Journal of Money, Credit and Banking,* 5, 1973; Roy Harrod, *Dynamic Economics* (especially pp. 80-84); Phyllis Deane, "Inflation in History," in David Heathfield, ed., *Perspectives on Inflation, Models and Policies;* and W. W. Rostow's article in *Inflation,* an anonymously edited volume published by Platform Books. For an early remarking of the parallels between the sixteenth- and twentieth-century price explosions, see page 76 of Kevin Phillips's *Mediacracy: American Parties and Politics in the Communications Age;* for a fuller account, see his *Post-Conservative America.* For another attempt to find an underlying theme in the four price explosions, see David Hackett Fischer, "Chronic Inflation: The Long View," in the *Journal of the Institute for Socioeconomic Studies,* Autumn 1980. Keynes's remarks on his "escape" from the confusions of the Quantity Theory come in the French preface to *The General Theory.*

On the power of the Monopoly game to command assent, see Bertell Ollman, *Class Struggle Is the Name of the Game.* Ralph Anspach's forthcoming description of his victorious battles with Parker Brothers and its parent, General Mills Corporation, over the history of both the Monopoly game and the Anti-Monopoly game he invented promises to be excellent. Presumably fresh from a big settlement, Anspach hasn't yet settled on a publisher. With regard to diffusion, see E. R. A. Seligman, "The Equal-Diffusion Theory," in *The Shifting and Incidence of Taxation,* and the entry "diffusion," in Palgrave's *Dictionary of Political Economy.* On revolution versus metamorphosis, see Gerhard O. Mensch, *Stalemate in Technology.* Stephen Jay

Gould's remarks on the nature of change were made in a letter published in the April 23, 1982, issue of *Science*. Cyril Stanley Smith's remarks are to be found in the essay "On Art, Invention and Technology" in his collected papers, *A Search for Structure*. The literature on money-tinkering is vast; not a bad starting point is William Poole, *Money and the Economy, A Monetarist View*. A paper on the economic history of the Weimar Republic that lays out the issues with special clarity is Charles P. Kindleberger, "A Structural View of the German Inflation," in the forthcoming *Inflation and Reconstruction in Germany and Europe: 1914-23*, edited by Gerald D. Feldman, Karl Holtfreich, C. A. Ritter, and Peter Witt. The splendid book in which the strato-inflation concept was proposed and an explanation offered is Dudley Jackson, H. A. Turner, and Frank Wilkinson, *Do Trade Unions Cause Inflation?* Descriptive material on the Family Budget Series is available from the U.S. Bureau of Labor Statistics.

5. THE COMPLEXITY HYPOTHESIS II

On English economic history, the literature is simply vast. To sort through it I have depended on G. R. Elton's bibliography, *Modern Historians on British History 1485-1945*, and on the periodization of *The New Cambridge Economic History*, volumes 1-8. Especially useful have been M. M. Postan, *The Medieval Economy and Society: An Economic History of Britain in the Middle Ages;* Robert S. Lopez, *The Commercial Revolution of the Middle Ages;* Harry A. Miskamin, *The Economy of Early Renaissance Europe;* Lawrence Stone, *The Crisis of the Aristocracy: 1558-1641;* Immanuel Wallerstein, *The Modern World System: Capitalist Agriculture and the Origins of the European World-Economy in the Sixteenth Century* and *The Modern World System II: Mercantilism and the Consolidation of the European World-Economy 1600-1750;* G. R. Elton, *The Tudor Revolution in Government;* D. C. Coleman, *The Economy of England: 1450-1750* (in which the long quotation of John Cary, the Bristol merchant, is to be found); Jan Devries, *The Economy of Europe in an Age of Crisis: 1600-1750;* Carlo M. Cippola, *Before the Industrial Revolution: European Economy and Society, 1000-1700;* Phyllis Deane, *The First Industrial Revolution;* David Landes, *Prometheus Unbound;* H. J. Habakkuk, *American and British Technology in the Nineteenth Century;* Paul David, *Technical Choice, Innovation and Economic Growth;* W. W. Rostow, *The British Economy in the 19th Century;* and A. E. Musson, *The Growth of British Industry.* The closest thing to an orthodox treatment of the same stretch of European history as is here interpreted by the complexity hypothesis may be found in a essay by William Parker, "European Development in Millennial Perspective," which was written for a festschrift for W. W. Rostow that was published in three volumes as *Economics in the Long View,* edited by Charles Kindleberger and Guido Di Tella; any reader who takes the time to consult these essays will understand why it is that, in the company of historical economists, I feel like a sportswriter in the locker room of a World Series team. W. Arthur Lewis's comparison of episodes of rising prices in 1899-1913 and 1950-1979 is in the *Scandinavian Journal of Economics,* volume 82, number 4, 1980. The elegant and shrewd industry-by-industry examination of the English economy in the twentieth century by Peter Pagnamenta and Robin Overy, *All Our Working Lives,* based on the British Broadcasting Corporation series of the same name, is especially worth consulting, as is Charles Kindleberger's magisterial *A Financial History of Western Europe.* Both books were forthcoming as this one went to press.

On Earl Hamilton's thesis, see Hamilton's "American Treasure and the Rise of Capitalism," in the *Economica,* 1929; "Profit Inflation and the Industrial Revolution, 1751-1800," in the *Quarterly Journal of Economics,* 1942; "Prices and Progress," in the *Journal of Economic History,* 1952; and the enthusiastic gloss of Hamilton's first paper in John Maynard Keynes, *Treatise on Money,* volume 2. For criticism of Hamilton's thesis, see John U. Nef, "Prices and Industrial Capitalism in France and England, 1540-1640," in the *Economic History Review*, 1936-37; and David Felix, "Profit Inflation and Industrial Growth: The Historic Record and Contemporary Analogies," in the *Quarterly Journal of Economics*, August 1956. François Simiand's books are, as far as I know, untranslated. They are: *Récherches anciennes et nouvelles sur le mouvement général des prix 16e au 19e siècle* and *Les Fluctuations économiques à longue periode et la crise mondiale*. They are discussed briefly in the introduction to *Economy and Society in Early Modern Europe*, edited by Peter Burke. For a pair of books that approach price revolutions differently from this book, see Geoffrey Maynard, *Economic Development and the Price Level;* and Bela Cszikos-Nagy, *Towards a New Price Revolution*. For the flavor of tax push and growth of government arguments about rising prices, see John H. Hotson, *Stagflation and the Bastard Keynesians;* William Krehm, *Babel's Tower: The Dynamics of Economic Breakdown;* Robert Bacon and Walter Eltis, *Britain's Economic Problem: Too Few Producers;* or Jude Wanniski, *The Way the World Works*. Assar Lindbecks's analysis can be found in the *American Economic Review*, May 1983. Fernand Braudel's remarks on "staircases" are in a little volume of his lectures, *Afterthoughts on Material Civilization and Capitalism*. Brief commentaries on the complexity hypothesis are in George Gilder, *Wealth and Poverty;* and in Kevin Phillips, *Post-Conservative America*.

6. CONCRETE PICTURES

The use of the word "paradigm" in its modern sense arose from Thomas Kuhn, *The Structure of Scientific Revolutions*. The subject was pursued, among many other places, in Margaret Masterman's essay on paradigms in *Criticism and the Growth of Knowledge*, edited by Imre Lakatos and Alan Musgrave. An extremely interesting approach to the nature of economic knowledge, fundamentally different from this one, may be found in Donald McClosky's essay, "The Rhetoric of Economics," in the *Journal of Economic Literature*, June 1983. Good general introductions to the history of economic thought include Phyllis Deane, *The Evolution of Economic Ideas*, and Joseph Schumpeter, *History of Economic Analysis*. Introductions to the idea of general equilibrium may be found in Kenneth Arrow's article on the topic or in William Jaffe's essay on Leon Walras in the *International Encyclopedia of the Social Sciences*; as well as in Alfred Marshall, *Principles of Economics*, 24th edition; and in Gary Becker, *Economic Theory*. Introductions to the quantity theory may be found in Milton Friedman's article on the Quantity Theory in *The International Encyclopedia of the Social Sciences* (1968); as well as in Irving Fisher, *The Purchasing Power of Money*; and in Stephen W. Rousseas, *Monetary Theory*. What is still a fine picture of the classical dichotomy can be seen in D. H. Robertson's *Money* and H. D. Henderson's *Supply and Demand*. A fine description of the Boyle experiments is in one chapter of Rom Harré's *Great Scientific Experiments* and a convenient account of the Newtonian revolution is Richard Westfall, *The Construction of Modern Science;* I. Bernard Cohen's fascinating *The Newtonian Revolution* also covers the topic, at considerably greater depth. Oscar Morgenstern's remark on the fixed complexity of the heavens was made in "Descriptive, Predictive and Normative Theory," in *Kyklos* 25, no. 4, 1972. John Maynard Keynes's observations are in his essay on Marshall in *Essays in Biography*. The observation on the connection between the Quantity Theory and Boyle's Law is in the chapter "The Nature of Inflation," in G. L. S. Shackle, *The Nature of Economic Thought*. Parallels between the description of computers and the economy are explored in Peter Albin, *The Analysis of Complex Socioeconomic Systems*. Janos Kornai's major work is available in translation as *Anti-Equilibrium*.

7. COMPLEXITY AND FRAGILITY

Ecological fragility is discussed in two reviews by Robert M. May: "The Structure of Food Webs," in *Nature* 301, February 17, 1983; and "Food Webs," in *Science* 220, April 15, 1983. Hypotheses about social and economic fragility include Amory and Hunter Lovins, *Brittle Power;* Hyman Minsky, *Can "It" Happen Again? Essays on Instability and Finance;* and Felix Rohatyn, *The Twenty Year Century: Essays on Economics and Public Finance.* Some main long-wave sources are Joseph Schumpeter, *Business Cycles;* W. W. Rostow, *The World Economy: History and Prospect;* Jay W. Forrester, "Innovation and Economic Change," in *Futures,* August 1981; Gerhard Mensch, *Stalemate in Technology;* Christopher Freeman, John Clark, and Luc Soete, *Unemployment and Technological Innovation: A Study of Long Waves and Economic Development;* and Robert C. Beckman, *The Downwave.* Good discussions of current attitudes toward the Kondratieff wave are in David Dickson, "Technology and Cycles of Boom and Bust," in *Science* 219, February 25, 1983; as well as in papers by Edwin Mansfield, "Long Waves and Technical Innovation," and Nathan Rosenberg and Claudio R. Frischtak, "Long Waves and Economic Growth: A Critical Appraisal," both in the *American Economic Review* for May 1983; and finally in "A Technology Lag That May Stifle Growth," *Business Week,* October 11, 1982.

Analyses of the causes of the Great Depression proceed from Milton Friedman and Anna Schwartz, *A Monetary History of the United States, 1867-1960,* and include Charles P. Kindleberger, *The World in Depression, 1929-1939;* Peter Temin, *Did Monetary Forces Cause the Great Depression;* and *The Great Depression Revisited,* edited by Karl Brunner. Kindleberger's classification scheme was proposed in *Manias, Panics and Crashes* and was discussed in *Financial Crises,* edited by Kindleberger and Jean-Pierre Laffargue, while Minsky is discussed in *Financial Crises: Institutions and Markets in a Fragile Environment,* edited by Edward Altman and Arnold Sametz. Imaginative discussions of circumstances that might cause complexity to decrease are Paul Hawken, *The Next Economy*, and Ivan Illich, *Towards a History of Needs*, while Jean-Paul Sartre provided many arguments why diminished complexity would be desirable.

8. CONCLUSION

Books that offer general reasons for the rise of complexity include Douglass North and Robert P. Thomas, *The Rise of the West;* Douglass North, *Structure and Change in Economic History;* Mancur Olson, *The Rise and Decline of Nations;* Ester Boserup, *Population and Technological Change;* W. W. Rostow, *The World Economy: History and Prospect;* John U. Nef, *War and Human Progress;* Immanuel Wallerstein, *The Capitalist World Economy*; Perry Anderson, *Lineages of the Absolutist State;* Simon Kuznets, *Towards a Theory of Economic Growth;* John Hicks, *A Theory of Economic History;* Edward F. Denison, *Why Growth Rates Differ: Postwar Experience in Nine Western Countries;* Eric Jones, *The European Miracle*; and William H. McNeill, *The Pursuit of Power* and *Plagues and People*. The book *IBM and the U.S. Data Processing Industry*, by Franklin M. Fisher, John W. McKie, and Richard Mancke, affords insights into the growth of the computer industry. Jonathan Kaufman's pathbreaking article, "How NASA Helped Industry," appeared in the *Wall Street Journal*, August 28, 1981. Conventional analyses of the origins of "inflation" in the 1970s are Alan S. Blinder, *Economic Policy and the Great Stagflation*, and Otto Eckstein, *Core Inflation*, updated by each of the authors respectively in "The Anatomy of Double Digit Inflation in the 1970s" (National Bureau of Economic Research Working Paper 414, September 1983) and "Disinflation" (Data Resources Economic Studies No. 114, October 1983). For the pioneering work on dual labor markets, see Robert Averitt, *The Dual Economy*, and for imaginative discussions of the tendency of modern technology to produce a global dual economy, see Peter Albin, *Progress Without Poverty*, and Michael Piore and Suzanne Berger, *Dualism and Discontinuity in Industrial Design*. For a fuller discussion of wage history, see E. H. Phelps Brown, *The Inequality of Pay*. William H. McNeill's speculations are contained in *The Human Condition: An Ecological and Historical View*. Theodore Levitt's advice to executives appeared in *Fortune* for December 18, 1978, in the article "A Heretical View of Management 'Science.' " For an appropriate stance toward the future, see Robert Frost's *Collected Poems* and especially "Why Wait for Science?"

INDEX